TEACHER'S PET PUBLICATIONS

PUZZLE PACK
for
Animal Farm
based on the book by
George Orwell

Written by
William T. Collins

© 2005 Teacher's Pet Publications
All Rights Reserved

The materials in this packet are copyrighted
by Teacher's Pet Publications, Inc.

These pages may be duplicated by the purchaser
for use in the purchaser's own classroom.

Copying any of these materials and distributing them
for any other purpose is a violation of the copyright laws.

© 2005 Teacher's Pet Publications, Inc.
www.tpet.com

INTRODUCTION
If you already own the LitPlan for this title, this Puzzle Pack will refresh your Unit Resource Materials and Vocabulary Resource Materials sections plus give you additional materials you can substitute into the tests. If you do not already have a complete LitPlan, these pages will give you some supplemental materials to use with your own plan. There are two main groups of materials: one set for unit words (such as characters' names, symbols, places, etc.) and one set for vocabulary words associated with the book.

WORD LIST
There is a word list for both the unit words and the vocabulary words. These lists show you which words are being used in the materials and the clues or definitions being used for those words. You may want to give students a word list with clues/definitions to help them, or you may want students to only have a word list (without clues/definitions) if you want them to work a little harder. Both are available for duplication. The word lists can also be your "calling key" for the bingo games.

FILL IN THE BLANK AND MATCHING
There are 4 each of the fill in the blank and matching worksheets for both the unit and vocabulary words. These pages can be used either as extra worksheets for students or as objective parts of a unit test. They can be done individually if students need extra help or as a whole class activity to review the material covered.

MAGIC SQUARES
The magic squares not only reinforce the material covered but also work on reasoning and math skills. Many teachers have told us that their students really enjoy doing these!

WORD SEARCH PUZZLES
The word search words go in all directions, as indicated on your answer keys. Two of the word search puzzles have the clues listed rather than the words. This makes the puzzle a little more difficult, but it reinforces the material better. Two word search puzzles have words only for students who find the clue puzzles too difficult.

CROSSWORD PUZZLES
Both unit and vocabulary word sections have 4 crossword puzzles.

BINGO CARDS
There are 32 individual bingo cards for the unit words and 32 individual bingo cards for the vocabulary words. You can use your word list as a "call list," calling the words at random and marking them off of your list as you go, or you could use the flash cards by cutting them apart and drawing the words at random from a hat (or box or whatever). To make a better review, you might ask for the definition and spelling of each word as you call it out–or you could call out the definitions and have students tell you the words they need to look for on the puzzle.

JUGGLE LETTERS
The vocabulary juggle letter game is intended to help students learn the spellings of the words. One sheet has the definitions listed on it as an extra help for students who need it or to reinforce the definitions if you choose to do so.

FLASH CARDS
We've included a set of vocabulary flash cards you can duplicate, cut, and fold for your students. Some teachers make a few sets for general use by the class; others make a set for each student. Some teachers duplicate them for each student and have the students cut & fold their own. You can cut out just the words and put them in a hat, have each student pick out one word and write the definition and a sentence for that word. Students then swap words and papers, with the next student adding a sentence of his own under the last one. You can have students swap as many times as you like. Each time the student will read the sentences written prior to his own and then add a sentence. You can cut out the words and definitions separately and play "I Have; Who Has?" Each student in the room draws a word and definition. The first student says, "I have (the name of the word). Who has the definition?" The student with the definition reads it then says, "I have (the name of the vocabulary word she has). Who has the definition?" The round continues until all words and definitions have been given.

Animal Farm Word List

No.	Word	Clue/Definition
1.	ANIMAL	---- Farm
2.	APPLES	The pigs ate these and drank the milk
3.	BARN	Place of shelter for animals
4.	BATTLE	--- of the Cowshed
5.	BEASTS	----- of England
6.	BEDS	Pigs began to sleep in these
7.	BENJAMIN	Donkey
8.	BOXER	Huge, strong horse who had two maxims
9.	BROTHERS	All animals are equal; they are --------
10.	CLEVER	Smart; astute
11.	CLOVER	Motherly horse
12.	COMMANDMENTS	The animals lived by seven of these
13.	COMMITTEE	Decisions were made by ---s of pigs
14.	COMRADE	Means friend or fellow worker
15.	COW	The Battle of the ---shed
16.	DEBATE	Argument with rules
17.	DICTATOR	One single ruler with total power
18.	DOGS	Napoleon's guard animals
19.	EGGS	The hens had to give these up for sale
20.	ENEMY	Foe
21.	ENGLAND	Beasts of ----
22.	EQUAL	All animals are -----
23.	EXECUTE	Kill
24.	FABLE	Story in which animals speak & act like humans
25.	FARM	Animal ----
26.	FENCES	These keep animals in a particular pasture
27.	FIELD	Place to plant crops
28.	FLAG	A material symbol; the animals had a green & white one
29.	FOOD	A shortage of it triggered the revolution
30.	FREDERICK	Efficient neighboring farmer
31.	FREE	Liberated
32.	FRIENDS	Boxer and Benjamin, for example
33.	GOAT	Scape-----
34.	GUARD	Job of the dogs
35.	GUNS	Men shot these at the animals
36.	HERO	Snowball was Animal ----, First Class
37.	HOOF	Boxer split his; also the flag had one on it
38.	HOUSE	The pigs moved in there
39.	IDEA	Thought
40.	JONES	Owner of Manor Farm
41.	LEADER	One in charge; Napoleon, for example
42.	LEGS	Four ---- good; two --- bad
43.	LIES	Untruths
44.	MAN	All the habits of --- are evil.
45.	MILK	The pigs drank this and ate the apples
46.	MOLLIE	Horse who liked ribbons
47.	MOSES	Told stories about Sugarcandy Mountain
48.	NAPOLEON	Our Leader; the leader of the animals
49.	OLD	____ Major; his vision inspired the revolution
50.	ORWELL	Author
51.	PERSUADE	Win to another point of view

Animal Farm Word List

No. Word	Clue/Definition
52. PIGS	The cleverest of animals
53. POOR	Not wealthy
54. POWER	Influence; strength
55. RAVEN	Moses was one
56. RETIRE	Stop working after a period of time
57. REVOLUTION	Old Major forsaw the -----; uprising
58. SHEEP	The wooly animals
59. SHEETS	Use of these was forbidden, not the use of beds
60. SNOWBALL	The dogs chased him off of the farm
61. SQUEALER	The persuasive pig
62. STONES	Boxer carried tons of these to make the windmill
63. SUGAR	Sweet treat
64. SYMBOL	A sign; something that represents something else
65. TACTICS	Strategies
66. TRUE	Not a lie; correct
67. UTOPIA	A perfect society
68. VISION	Old Major had one of these
69. VOTE	An individual casts one in an election
70. WALL	Where the Seven Commandments were written
71. WHIP	Snappy implement used to hit horses
72. WHISKEY	The pigs found a case of this and drank too much
73. WHYMPER	Middleman between Animal Farm & human world
74. WINDMILL	Snowball and Napoleon disagreed about building it
75. WORK	Duties; opposite of play
76. WRITE	Most animals learned to read and ---

Animal Farm Fill In The Blank 1

Fill in the blank with the term that is described.

_____ 1. The animals lived by seven of these

_____ 2. One single ruler with total power

_____ 3. Snappy implement used to hit horses

_____ 4. ----- of England

_____ 5. Four ---- good; two --- bad

_____ 6. Strategies

_____ 7. Argument with rules

_____ 8. A material symbol; the animals had a green & white one

_____ 9. The cleverest of animals

_____ 10. The Battle of the ---shed

_____ 11. Foe

_____ 12. The dogs chased him off of the farm

_____ 13. All the habits of --- are evil.

_____ 14. Influence; strength

_____ 15. Huge, strong horse who had two maxims

_____ 16. An individual casts one in an election

_____ 17. Donkey

_____ 18. Place of shelter for animals

_____ 19. Snowball was Animal ----, First Class

_____ 20. Motherly horse

Animal Farm Fill In The Blank 1 Answer Key

COMMANDMENTS	1. The animals lived by seven of these
DICTATOR	2. One single ruler with total power
WHIP	3. Snappy implement used to hit horses
BEASTS	4. ----- of England
LEGS	5. Four ---- good; two --- bad
TACTICS	6. Strategies
DEBATE	7. Argument with rules
FLAG	8. A material symbol; the animals had a green & white one
PIGS	9. The cleverest of animals
COW	10. The Battle of the ---shed
ENEMY	11. Foe
SNOWBALL	12. The dogs chased him off of the farm
MAN	13. All the habits of --- are evil.
POWER	14. Influence; strength
BOXER	15. Huge, strong horse who had two maxims
VOTE	16. An individual casts one in an election
BENJAMIN	17. Donkey
BARN	18. Place of shelter for animals
HERO	19. Snowball was Animal ----, First Class
CLOVER	20. Motherly horse

Animal Farm Fill In The Blank 2

Fill in the blank with the term that is described.

_____ 1. Means friend or fellow worker

_____ 2. Not a lie; correct

_____ 3. Where the Seven Commandments were written

_____ 4. Our Leader; the leader of the animals

_____ 5. The dogs chased him off of the farm

_____ 6. Boxer carried tons of these to make the windmill

_____ 7. Sweet treat

_____ 8. Napoleon's guard animals

_____ 9. Untruths

_____ 10. Influence; strength

_____ 11. The hens had to give these up for sale

_____ 12. Story in which animals speak & act like humans

_____ 13. A sign; something that represents something else

_____ 14. Told stories about Sugarcandy Mountain

_____ 15. Use of these was forbidden, not the use of beds

_____ 16. The cleverest of animals

_____ 17. A perfect society

_____ 18. Efficient neighboring farmer

_____ 19. Job of the dogs

_____ 20. These keep animals in a particular pasture

Animal Farm Fill In The Blank 2 Answer Key

Fill in the blank with the term that is described.

COMRADE	1. Means friend or fellow worker
TRUE	2. Not a lie; correct
WALL	3. Where the Seven Commandments were written
NAPOLEON	4. Our Leader; the leader of the animals
SNOWBALL	5. The dogs chased him off of the farm
STONES	6. Boxer carried tons of these to make the windmill
SUGAR	7. Sweet treat
DOGS	8. Napoleon's guard animals
LIES	9. Untruths
POWER	10. Influence; strength
EGGS	11. The hens had to give these up for sale
FABLE	12. Story in which animals speak & act like humans
SYMBOL	13. A sign; something that represents something else
MOSES	14. Told stories about Sugarcandy Mountain
SHEETS	15. Use of these was forbidden, not the use of beds
PIGS	16. The cleverest of animals
UTOPIA	17. A perfect society
FREDERICK	18. Efficient neighboring farmer
GUARD	19. Job of the dogs
FENCES	20. These keep animals in a particular pasture

Animal Farm Fill In The Blank 3

Fill in the blank with the term that is described.

_____ 1. Duties; opposite of play
_____ 2. Pigs began to sleep in these
_____ 3. Foe
_____ 4. Untruths
_____ 5. Horse who liked ribbons
_____ 6. Place to plant crops
_____ 7. The dogs chased him off of the farm
_____ 8. One single ruler with total power
_____ 9. Decisions were made by ---s of pigs
_____ 10. Snappy implement used to hit horses
_____ 11. Middleman between Animal Farm & human world
_____ 12. Boxer carried tons of these to make the windmill
_____ 13. A shortage of it triggered the revolution
_____ 14. Boxer split his; also the flag had one on it
_____ 15. Boxer and Benjamin, for example
_____ 16. Huge, strong horse who had two maxims
_____ 17. Men shot these at the animals
_____ 18. The persuasive pig
_____ 19. Napoleon's guard animals
_____ 20. All animals are equal; they are --------

Animal Farm Fill In The Blank 3 Answer Key

Answer	Clue
WORK	1. Duties; opposite of play
BEDS	2. Pigs began to sleep in these
ENEMY	3. Foe
LIES	4. Untruths
MOLLIE	5. Horse who liked ribbons
FIELD	6. Place to plant crops
SNOWBALL	7. The dogs chased him off of the farm
DICTATOR	8. One single ruler with total power
COMMITTEE	9. Decisions were made by ---s of pigs
WHIP	10. Snappy implement used to hit horses
WHYMPER	11. Middleman between Animal Farm & human world
STONES	12. Boxer carried tons of these to make the windmill
FOOD	13. A shortage of it triggered the revolution
HOOF	14. Boxer split his; also the flag had one on it
FRIENDS	15. Boxer and Benjamin, for example
BOXER	16. Huge, strong horse who had two maxims
GUNS	17. Men shot these at the animals
SQUEALER	18. The persuasive pig
DOGS	19. Napoleon's guard animals
BROTHERS	20. All animals are equal; they are --------

Animal Farm Fill In The Blank 4

Fill in the blank with the term that is described.

_____ 1. One in charge; Napoleon, for example

_____ 2. Four ---- good; two --- bad

_____ 3. Not a lie; correct

_____ 4. All animals are -----

_____ 5. Win to another point of view

_____ 6. ----- of England

_____ 7. The pigs ate these and drank the milk

_____ 8. Job of the dogs

_____ 9. Huge, strong horse who had two maxims

_____ 10. One single ruler with total power

_____ 11. Men shot these at the animals

_____ 12. Stop working after a period of time

_____ 13. --- of the Cowshed

_____ 14. His vision inspired the revolution

_____ 15. Place of shelter for animals

_____ 16. Motherly horse

_____ 17. Not wealthy

_____ 18. Boxer and Benjamin, for example

_____ 19. Duties; opposite of play

_____ 20. Scape-----

Animal Farm Fill In The Blank 4 Answer Key

LEADER	1. One in charge; Napoleon, for example
LEGS	2. Four ---- good; two --- bad
TRUE	3. Not a lie; correct
EQUAL	4. All animals are -----
PERSUADE	5. Win to another point of view
BEASTS	6. ----- of England
APPLES	7. The pigs ate these and drank the milk
GUARD	8. Job of the dogs
BOXER	9. Huge, strong horse who had two maxims
DICTATOR	10. One single ruler with total power
GUNS	11. Men shot these at the animals
RETIRE	12. Stop working after a period of time
BATTLE	13. --- of the Cowshed
OLD	14. ____Major; his vision inspired the revolution
BARN	15. Place of shelter for animals
CLOVER	16. Motherly horse
POOR	17. Not wealthy
FRIENDS	18. Boxer and Benjamin, for example
WORK	19. Duties; opposite of play
GOAT	20. Scape-----

Animal Farm Matching 1

___ 1. TACTICS   A. Our Leader; the leader of the animals
___ 2. ENEMY   B. Strategies
___ 3. FABLE   C. Moses was one
___ 4. SNOWBALL   D. The dogs chased him off of the farm
___ 5. WHISKEY   E. Middleman between Animal Farm & human world
___ 6. COMMITTEE   F. Boxer split his; also the flag had one on it
___ 7. UTOPIA   G. An individual casts one in an election
___ 8. HOOF   H. The pigs ate these and drank the milk
___ 9. NAPOLEON   I. Boxer and Benjamin, for example
___10. MAN   J. Story in which animals speak & act like humans
___11. WHYMPER   K. The pigs moved in there
___12. COMMANDMENTS   L. Not wealthy
___13. HOUSE   M. The animals lived by seven of these
___14. VOTE   N. Job of the dogs
___15. FRIENDS   O. The pigs drank this and ate the apples
___16. MOSES   P. A perfect society
___17. POOR   Q. Decisions were made by ---s of pigs
___18. RETIRE   R. Beasts of ----
___19. IDEA   S. Thought
___20. MILK   T. Stop working after a period of time
___21. ENGLAND   U. All the habits of --- are evil.
___22. APPLES   V. Foe
___23. BARN   W. Place of shelter for animals
___24. RAVEN   X. The pigs found a case of this and drank too much
___25. GUARD   Y. Told stories about Sugarcandy Mountain

Animal Farm Matching 1 Answer Key

B - 1.	TACTICS	A.	Our Leader; the leader of the animals
V - 2.	ENEMY	B.	Strategies
J - 3.	FABLE	C.	Moses was one
D - 4.	SNOWBALL	D.	The dogs chased him off of the farm
X - 5.	WHISKEY	E.	Middleman between Animal Farm & human world
Q - 6.	COMMITTEE	F.	Boxer split his; also the flag had one on it
P - 7.	UTOPIA	G.	An individual casts one in an election
F - 8.	HOOF	H.	The pigs ate these and drank the milk
A - 9.	NAPOLEON	I.	Boxer and Benjamin, for example
U -10.	MAN	J.	Story in which animals speak & act like humans
E -11.	WHYMPER	K.	The pigs moved in there
M -12.	COMMANDMENTS	L.	Not wealthy
K -13.	HOUSE	M.	The animals lived by seven of these
G -14.	VOTE	N.	Job of the dogs
I -15.	FRIENDS	O.	The pigs drank this and ate the apples
Y -16.	MOSES	P.	A perfect society
L -17.	POOR	Q.	Decisions were made by ---s of pigs
T -18.	RETIRE	R.	Beasts of ----
S -19.	IDEA	S.	Thought
O -20.	MILK	T.	Stop working after a period of time
R -21.	ENGLAND	U.	All the habits of --- are evil.
H -22.	APPLES	V.	Foe
W -23.	BARN	W.	Place of shelter for animals
C -24.	RAVEN	X.	The pigs found a case of this and drank too much
N -25.	GUARD	Y.	Told stories about Sugarcandy Mountain

Animal Farm Matching 2

___ 1. POOR
___ 2. PIGS
___ 3. BROTHERS
___ 4. WINDMILL
___ 5. RAVEN
___ 6. LIES
___ 7. BEASTS
___ 8. FIELD
___ 9. RETIRE
___10. FARM
___11. GOAT
___12. APPLES
___13. BEDS
___14. COW
___15. TACTICS
___16. CLOVER
___17. DEBATE
___18. FREDERICK
___19. ENGLAND
___20. BARN
___21. POWER
___22. IDEA
___23. HERO
___24. DICTATOR
___25. SHEETS

A. Use of these was forbidden, not the use of beds
B. Thought
C. Strategies
D. Influence; strength
E. All animals are equal; they are --------
F. Place to plant crops
G. Argument with rules
H. Pigs began to sleep in these
I. Not wealthy
J. Motherly horse
K. Efficient neighboring farmer
L. The pigs ate these and drank the milk
M. Untruths
N. Snowball was Animal ----, First Class
O. Place of shelter for animals
P. Animal ----
Q. ----- of England
R. Scape-----
S. Stop working after a period of time
T. Beasts of ----
U. The Battle of the ---shed
V. Snowball and Napoleon disagreed about building it
W. The cleverest of animals
X. One single ruler with total power
Y. Moses was one

Animal Farm Matching 2 Answer Key

I - 1. POOR	A.	Use of these was forbidden, not the use of beds
W - 2. PIGS	B.	Thought
E - 3. BROTHERS	C.	Strategies
V - 4. WINDMILL	D.	Influence; strength
Y - 5. RAVEN	E.	All animals are equal; they are --------
M - 6. LIES	F.	Place to plant crops
Q - 7. BEASTS	G.	Argument with rules
F - 8. FIELD	H.	Pigs began to sleep in these
S - 9. RETIRE	I.	Not wealthy
P -10. FARM	J.	Motherly horse
R -11. GOAT	K.	Efficient neighboring farmer
L -12. APPLES	L.	The pigs ate these and drank the milk
H -13. BEDS	M.	Untruths
U -14. COW	N.	Snowball was Animal ----, First Class
C -15. TACTICS	O.	Place of shelter for animals
J -16. CLOVER	P.	Animal ----
G -17. DEBATE	Q.	----- of England
K -18. FREDERICK	R.	Scape-----
T -19. ENGLAND	S.	Stop working after a period of time
O -20. BARN	T.	Beasts of ----
D -21. POWER	U.	The Battle of the ---shed
B -22. IDEA	V.	Snowball and Napoleon disagreed about building it
N -23. HERO	W.	The cleverest of animals
X -24. DICTATOR	X.	One single ruler with total power
A -25. SHEETS	Y.	Moses was one

Animal Farm Matching 3

___ 1. DEBATE   A. The pigs moved in there
___ 2. CLOVER   B. All animals are equal; they are --------
___ 3. RETIRE   C. Snappy implement used to hit horses
___ 4. EGGS   D. Four ---- good; two --- bad
___ 5. BOXER   E. Huge, strong horse who had two maxims
___ 6. POWER   F. The dogs chased him off of the farm
___ 7. STONES   G. Influence; strength
___ 8. WHIP   H. Boxer split his; also the flag had one on it
___ 9. UTOPIA   I. Duties; opposite of play
___10. HOOF   J. ----- of England
___11. NAPOLEON   K. Stop working after a period of time
___12. SNOWBALL   L. Motherly horse
___13. BROTHERS   M. The pigs ate these and drank the milk
___14. LEADER   N. Argument with rules
___15. BEASTS   O. Use of these was forbidden, not the use of beds
___16. FOOD   P. Our Leader; the leader of the animals
___17. SQUEALER   Q. Animal ----
___18. SHEETS   R. Strategies
___19. APPLES   S. The hens had to give these up for sale
___20. FREE   T. The persuasive pig
___21. HOUSE   U. One in charge; Napoleon, for example
___22. TACTICS   V. Boxer carried tons of these to make the windmill
___23. WORK   W. A perfect society
___24. LEGS   X. A shortage of it triggered the revolution
___25. FARM   Y. Liberated

Animal Farm Matching 3 Answer Key

N - 1.	DEBATE	A. The pigs moved in there
L - 2.	CLOVER	B. All animals are equal; they are --------
K - 3.	RETIRE	C. Snappy implement used to hit horses
S - 4.	EGGS	D. Four ---- good; two --- bad
E - 5.	BOXER	E. Huge, strong horse who had two maxims
G - 6.	POWER	F. The dogs chased him off of the farm
V - 7.	STONES	G. Influence; strength
C - 8.	WHIP	H. Boxer split his; also the flag had one on it
W - 9.	UTOPIA	I. Duties; opposite of play
H - 10.	HOOF	J. ----- of England
P - 11.	NAPOLEON	K. Stop working after a period of time
F - 12.	SNOWBALL	L. Motherly horse
B - 13.	BROTHERS	M. The pigs ate these and drank the milk
U - 14.	LEADER	N. Argument with rules
J - 15.	BEASTS	O. Use of these was forbidden, not the use of beds
X - 16.	FOOD	P. Our Leader; the leader of the animals
T - 17.	SQUEALER	Q. Animal ----
O - 18.	SHEETS	R. Strategies
M - 19.	APPLES	S. The hens had to give these up for sale
Y - 20.	FREE	T. The persuasive pig
A - 21.	HOUSE	U. One in charge; Napoleon, for example
R - 22.	TACTICS	V. Boxer carried tons of these to make the windmill
I - 23.	WORK	W. A perfect society
D - 24.	LEGS	X. A shortage of it triggered the revolution
Q - 25.	FARM	Y. Liberated

Animal Farm Matching 4

___ 1. STONES   A. Kill
___ 2. WHIP   B. Efficient neighboring farmer
___ 3. FENCES   C. The persuasive pig
___ 4. UTOPIA   D. Owner of Manor Farm
___ 5. SQUEALER   E. A perfect society
___ 6. FOOD   F. Strategies
___ 7. TACTICS   G. The dogs chased him off of the farm
___ 8. SHEEP   H. Not wealthy
___ 9. FREDERICK   I. The wooly animals
___10. VISION   J. Liberated
___11. WHYMPER   K. All animals are equal; they are --------
___12. NAPOLEON   L. Argument with rules
___13. VOTE   M. Sweet treat
___14. WINDMILL   N. A shortage of it triggered the revolution
___15. FLAG   O. Our Leader; the leader of the animals
___16. SUGAR   P. Old Major had one of these
___17. BROTHERS   Q. These keep animals in a particular pasture
___18. JONES   R. A material symbol; the animals had a green & white one
___19. FREE   S. Snappy implement used to hit horses
___20. DEBATE   T. Snowball and Napoleon disagreed about building it
___21. TRUE   U. Not a lie; correct
___22. SNOWBALL   V. Boxer carried tons of these to make the windmill
___23. PERSUADE   W. Middleman between Animal Farm & human world
___24. POOR   X. An individual casts one in an election
___25. EXECUTE   Y. Win to another point of view

Animal Farm Matching 4 Answer Key

V - 1.	STONES	A.	Kill
S - 2.	WHIP	B.	Efficient neighboring farmer
Q - 3.	FENCES	C.	The persuasive pig
E - 4.	UTOPIA	D.	Owner of Manor Farm
C - 5.	SQUEALER	E.	A perfect society
N - 6.	FOOD	F.	Strategies
F - 7.	TACTICS	G.	The dogs chased him off of the farm
I - 8.	SHEEP	H.	Not wealthy
B - 9.	FREDERICK	I.	The wooly animals
P - 10.	VISION	J.	Liberated
W - 11.	WHYMPER	K.	All animals are equal; they are --------
O - 12.	NAPOLEON	L.	Argument with rules
X - 13.	VOTE	M.	Sweet treat
T - 14.	WINDMILL	N.	A shortage of it triggered the revolution
R - 15.	FLAG	O.	Our Leader; the leader of the animals
M - 16.	SUGAR	P.	Old Major had one of these
K - 17.	BROTHERS	Q.	These keep animals in a particular pasture
D - 18.	JONES	R.	A material symbol; the animals had a green & white one
J - 19.	FREE	S.	Snappy implement used to hit horses
L - 20.	DEBATE	T.	Snowball and Napoleon disagreed about building it
U - 21.	TRUE	U.	Not a lie; correct
G - 22.	SNOWBALL	V.	Boxer carried tons of these to make the windmill
Y - 23.	PERSUADE	W.	Middleman between Animal Farm & human world
H - 24.	POOR	X.	An individual casts one in an election
A - 25.	EXECUTE	Y.	Win to another point of view

Animal Farm Magic Squares 1

Match the definition with the vocabulary word. Put your answers in the magic squares below. When your answers are correct, all columns and rows will add to the same number.

A. NAPOLEON   G. WHIP   M. FIELD
B. EQUAL   H. WRITE   N. RETIRE
C. POWER   I. BEASTS   O. IDEA
D. GUARD   J. EXECUTE   P. ORWELL
E. ENGLAND   K. COMMANDMENTS
F. MAN   L. LIES

1. All animals are -----
2. Snappy implement used to hit horses
3. The animals lived by seven of these
4. Stop working after a period of time
5. Place to plant crops
6. Untruths
7. Most animals learned to read and ---
8. Our Leader; the leader of the animals

9. Author
10. ----- of England
11. Beasts of ----
12. Job of the dogs
13. Influence; strength
14. All the habits of --- are evil.
15. Kill
16. Thought

A=	B=	C=	D=
E=	F=	G=	H=
I=	J=	K=	L=
M=	N=	O=	P=

22
Copyrighted

Animal Farm Magic Squares 1 Answer Key

Match the definition with the vocabulary word. Put your answers in the magic squares below. When your answers are correct, all columns and rows will add to the same number.

A. NAPOLEON
B. EQUAL
C. POWER
D. GUARD
E. ENGLAND
F. MAN
G. WHIP
H. WRITE
I. BEASTS
J. EXECUTE
K. COMMANDMENTS
L. LIES
M. FIELD
N. RETIRE
O. IDEA
P. ORWELL

1. All animals are -----
2. Snappy implement used to hit horses
3. The animals lived by seven of these
4. Stop working after a period of time
5. Place to plant crops
6. Untruths
7. Most animals learned to read and ---
8. Our Leader; the leader of the animals
9. Author
10. ----- of England
11. Beasts of ----
12. Job of the dogs
13. Influence; strength
14. All the habits of --- are evil.
15. Kill
16. Thought

A=8	B=1	C=13	D=12
E=11	F=14	G=2	H=7
I=10	J=15	K=3	L=6
M=5	N=4	O=16	P=9

Animal Farm Magic Squares 2

Match the definition with the vocabulary word. Put your answers in the magic squares below. When your answers are correct, all columns and rows will add to the same number.

A. WALL
B. POOR
C. WHISKEY
D. FENCES
E. REVOLUTION
F. EXECUTE
G. CLEVER
H. FREDERICK
I. BENJAMIN
J. ENGLAND
K. BOXER
L. LEGS
M. HOOF
N. WHYMPER
O. RAVEN
P. DOGS

1. Not wealthy
2. Smart; astute
3. Huge, strong horse who had two maxims
4. Middleman between Animal Farm & human world
5. Boxer split his; also the flag had one on it
6. Four ---- good; two --- bad
7. Efficient neighboring farmer
8. Where the Seven Commandments were written
9. Napoleon's guard animals
10. Donkey
11. Old Major forsaw the -----; uprising
12. These keep animals in a particular pasture
13. The pigs found a case of this and drank too much
14. Kill
15. Beasts of ----
16. Moses was one

A=	B=	C=	D=
E=	F=	G=	H=
I=	J=	K=	L=
M=	N=	O=	P=

Animal Farm Magic Squares 2 Answer Key

Match the definition with the vocabulary word. Put your answers in the magic squares below. When your answers are correct, all columns and rows will add to the same number.

A. WALL
B. POOR
C. WHISKEY
D. FENCES
E. REVOLUTION
F. EXECUTE
G. CLEVER
H. FREDERICK
I. BENJAMIN
J. ENGLAND
K. BOXER
L. LEGS
M. HOOF
N. WHYMPER
O. RAVEN
P. DOGS

1. Not wealthy
2. Smart; astute
3. Huge, strong horse who had two maxims
4. Middleman between Animal Farm & human world
5. Boxer split his; also the flag had one on it
6. Four ---- good; two --- bad
7. Efficient neighboring farmer
8. Where the Seven Commandments were written
9. Napoleon's guard animals
10. Donkey
11. Old Major forsaw the -----; uprising
12. These keep animals in a particular pasture
13. The pigs found a case of this and drank too much
14. Kill
15. Beasts of ----
16. Moses was one

A=8	B=1	C=13	D=12
E=11	F=14	G=2	H=7
I=10	J=15	K=3	L=6
M=5	N=4	O=16	P=9

Animal Farm Magic Squares 3

Match the definition with the vocabulary word. Put your answers in the magic squares below. When your answers are correct, all columns and rows will add to the same number.

A. GOAT
B. SUGAR
C. SHEEP
D. WINDMILL
E. LIES
F. RAVEN

G. VISION
H. GUNS
I. FARM
J. VOTE
K. BEDS
L. FREDERICK

M. MAN
N. CLOVER
O. COMMITTEE
P. DOGS

1. Sweet treat
2. Old Major had one of these
3. Pigs began to sleep in these
4. Motherly horse
5. All the habits of --- are evil.
6. Efficient neighboring farmer
7. Men shot these at the animals
8. Scape-----
9. Napoleon's guard animals
10. Animal ----
11. Untruths
12. Snowball and Napoleon disagreed about building it
13. The wooly animals
14. Moses was one
15. An individual casts one in an election
16. Decisions were made by ---s of pigs

A=	B=	C=	D=
E=	F=	G=	H=
I=	J=	K=	L=
M=	N=	O=	P=

Animal Farm Magic Squares 3 Answer Key

Match the definition with the vocabulary word. Put your answers in the magic squares below. When your answers are correct, all columns and rows will add to the same number.

A. GOAT
B. SUGAR
C. SHEEP
D. WINDMILL
E. LIES
F. RAVEN
G. VISION
H. GUNS
I. FARM
J. VOTE
K. BEDS
L. FREDERICK
M. MAN
N. CLOVER
O. COMMITTEE
P. DOGS

1. Sweet treat
2. Old Major had one of these
3. Pigs began to sleep in these
4. Motherly horse
5. All the habits of --- are evil.
6. Efficient neighboring farmer
7. Men shot these at the animals
8. Scape-----
9. Napoleon's guard animals
10. Animal ----
11. Untruths
12. Snowball and Napoleon disagreed about building it
13. The wooly animals
14. Moses was one
15. An individual casts one in an election
16. Decisions were made by ---s of pigs

A=8	B=1	C=13	D=12
E=11	F=14	G=2	H=7
I=10	J=15	K=3	L=6
M=5	N=4	O=16	P=9

Animal Farm Magic Squares 4

Match the definition with the vocabulary word. Put your answers in the magic squares below. When your answers are correct, all columns and rows will add to the same number.

A. WALL
B. COMMITTEE
C. FENCES
D. POOR
E. STONES
F. TRUE
G. FARM
H. REVOLUTION
I. IDEA
J. DICTATOR
K. NAPOLEON
L. BEDS
M. LEADER
N. DEBATE
O. LIES
P. BOXER

1. Not a lie; correct
2. Thought
3. Untruths
4. Not wealthy
5. One in charge; Napoleon, for example
6. Decisions were made by ---s of pigs
7. Old Major forsaw the -----; uprising
8. Our Leader; the leader of the animals
9. These keep animals in a particular pasture
10. Huge, strong horse who had two maxims
11. One single ruler with total power
12. Boxer carried tons of these to make the windmill
13. Pigs began to sleep in these
14. Animal ----
15. Where the Seven Commandments were written
16. Argument with rules

A=	B=	C=	D=
E=	F=	G=	H=
I=	J=	K=	L=
M=	N=	O=	P=

Copyrighted

Animal Farm Magic Squares 4 Answer Key

Match the definition with the vocabulary word. Put your answers in the magic squares below. When your answers are correct, all columns and rows will add to the same number.

A. WALL
B. COMMITTEE
C. FENCES
D. POOR
E. STONES
F. TRUE
G. FARM
H. REVOLUTION
I. IDEA
J. DICTATOR
K. NAPOLEON
L. BEDS
M. LEADER
N. DEBATE
O. LIES
P. BOXER

1. Not a lie; correct
2. Thought
3. Untruths
4. Not wealthy
5. One in charge; Napoleon, for example
6. Decisions were made by ---s of pigs
7. Old Major forsaw the -----; uprising
8. Our Leader; the leader of the animals
9. These keep animals in a particular pasture
10. Huge, strong horse who had two maxims
11. One single ruler with total power
12. Boxer carried tons of these to make the windmill
13. Pigs began to sleep in these
14. Animal ----
15. Where the Seven Commandments were written
16. Argument with rules

A=15	B=6	C=9	D=4
E=12	F=1	G=14	H=7
I=2	J=11	K=8	L=13
M=5	N=16	O=3	P=10

Animal Farm Word Search 1

```
W H I S K E Y B M G U N S S F I E L D L
O H E M S T E C O I I Y E D U A E G O M
C I E U G A W A O M L L C N N G R W G H
L P O R S B T J A M P K N E S F A M S S
A H O T O E O J O P M E E I M L E R W M
M K S O F D N X A N V A F R L C D H R R
I U K E R E P N E A E C N F W R I T E T
N Z T A B E A N R R N S O D O P Q L T H
A O U O E M E L G B G Y I M M O A E I M
V G H H P M W L Y K L M S V M E D U R R
Q B S O Y I B A R N A B I P U I N R E Y
P G A S O C A B Q M N O V Q I H T K B
G O D T G F Z W H L D L S Y F G V T S G
G E W A T J T O O L E A D E R H S Q E N
B P L E M L H N O R W E L L E L B A F E
X F R F R Z E S W Q K S H E E T S C L S
```

--- of the Cowshed (6)
---- Farm (6)
----- of England (6)
A material symbol; the animals had a green & white one (4)
A perfect society (6)
A shortage of it triggered the revolution (4)
A sign; something that represents something else (6)
All the habits of --- are evil. (3)
An individual casts one in an election (4)
Animal ---- (4)
Argument with rules (6)
Author (6)
Beasts of ---- (7)
Boxer and Benjamin, for example (7)
Boxer split his; also the flag had one on it (4)
Decisions were made by ---s of pigs (9)
Donkey (8)
Duties; opposite of play (4)
Foe (5)
Four ---- good; two --- bad (4)
Huge, strong horse who had two maxims (5)
Influence; strength (5)
Job of the dogs (5)
Liberated (4)
Men shot these at the animals (4)
Moses was one (5)
Most animals learned to read and --- (5)
Napoleon's guard animals (4)
Not a lie; correct (4)
Not wealthy (4)

Old Major had one of these (6)
One in charge; Napoleon, for example (6)
Owner of Manor Farm (5)
Pigs began to sleep in these (4)
Place of shelter for animals (4)
Place to plant crops (5)
Scape----- (4)
Snappy implement used to hit horses (4)
Snowball was Animal ----, First Class (4)
Stop working after a period of time (6)
Story in which animals speak & act like humans (5)
Sweet treat (5)
The Battle of the ---shed (3)
The animals lived by seven of these (12)
The cleverest of animals (4)
The dogs chased him off of the farm (8)
The hens had to give these up for sale (4)
The persuasive pig (8)
The pigs ate these and drank the milk (6)
The pigs drank this and ate the apples (4)
The pigs found a case of this and drank too much (7)
The pigs moved in there (5)
The wooly animals (5)
These keep animals in a particular pasture (6)
Thought (4)
Untruths (4)
Use of these was forbidden, not the use of beds (6)
Where the Seven Commandments were written (4)

Animal Farm Word Search 1 Answer Key

--- of the Cowshed (6)
---- Farm (6)
----- of England (6)
A material symbol; the animals had a green & white one (4)
A perfect society (6)
A shortage of it triggered the revolution (4)
A sign; something that represents something else (6)
All the habits of --- are evil. (3)
An individual casts one in an election (4)
Animal ---- (4)
Argument with rules (6)
Author (6)
Beasts of ---- (7)
Boxer and Benjamin, for example (7)
Boxer split his; also the flag had one on it (4)
Decisions were made by ---s of pigs (9)
Donkey (8)
Duties; opposite of play (4)
Foe (5)
Four ---- good; two --- bad (4)
Huge, strong horse who had two maxims (5)
Influence; strength (5)
Job of the dogs (5)
Liberated (4)
Men shot these at the animals (4)
Moses was one (5)
Most animals learned to read and --- (5)
Napoleon's guard animals (4)
Not a lie; correct (4)
Not wealthy (4)

Old Major had one of these (6)
One in charge; Napoleon, for example (6)
Owner of Manor Farm (5)
Pigs began to sleep in these (4)
Place of shelter for animals (4)
Place to plant crops (5)
Scape----- (4)
Snappy implement used to hit horses (4)
Snowball was Animal ----, First Class (4)
Stop working after a period of time (6)
Story in which animals speak & act like humans (5)
Sweet treat (5)
The Battle of the ---shed (3)
The animals lived by seven of these (12)
The cleverest of animals (4)
The dogs chased him off of the farm (8)
The hens had to give these up for sale (4)
The persuasive pig (8)
The pigs ate these and drank the milk (6)
The pigs drank this and ate the apples (4)
The pigs found a case of this and drank too much (7)
The pigs moved in there (5)
The wooly animals (5)
These keep animals in a particular pasture (6)
Thought (4)
Untruths (4)
Use of these was forbidden, not the use of beds (6)
Where the Seven Commandments were written (4)

Animal Farm Word Search 2

```
E G G S N I M A J N E B T V W H L E P Q
W X B E D S T R N F G A O O O L O Q I K
I N E K N H A E D I B R C X A T Y U G Q
N O L C W R I T E K M N B E E E A S Q H
D I F S U L T I S W Y A W M D R Q L S E
M S E L M T R R G Y H O L A D S E Q T R
I I K E R W E E O U N I R T S U X P N W
L V M A N B V J D S N M P E R S S G E L
L G G D O R O O F Y O S S T R A N M R
D U U E R O L N M C F O D E O L G A D V
S A T R W T C E C E M N E T F W E P N J
C R O C E H N S N D A H A H K I L O A H
G D P P L E Z C N L S T P H L W B L M H
Q O I L L R E Z G E C X O L E O A E M C
B E A S T S D N E I R F O E E R F O O D
N W S T O N E S D F Z M R A F K O N C K
```

---- Farm (6)
----- of England (6)
A material symbol; the animals had a green & white one (4)
A perfect society (6)
A shortage of it triggered the revolution (4)
All animals are ----- (5)
All animals are equal; they are -------- (8)
All the habits of --- are evil. (3)
An individual casts one in an election (4)
Animal ---- (4)
Author (6)
Beasts of ---- (7)
Boxer and Benjamin, for example (7)
Boxer carried tons of these to make the windmill (6)
Donkey (8)
Duties; opposite of play (4)
Foe (5)
Four ---- good; two --- bad (4)
Horse who liked ribbons (6)
Huge, strong horse who had two maxims (5)
Job of the dogs (5)
Kill (7)
Liberated (4)
Means friend or fellow worker (7)
Men shot these at the animals (4)
Most animals learned to read and --- (5)
Motherly horse (6)
Napoleon's guard animals (4)
Not a lie; correct (4)
Not wealthy (4)

Old Major had one of these (6)
One in charge; Napoleon, for example (6)
One single ruler with total power (8)
Our Leader; the leader of the animals (8)
Owner of Manor Farm (5)
Pigs began to sleep in these (4)
Place of shelter for animals (4)
Place to plant crops (5)
Scape----- (4)
Snappy implement used to hit horses (4)
Snowball and Napoleon disagreed about building it (8)
Snowball was Animal ----, First Class (4)
Stop working after a period of time (6)
Story in which animals speak & act like humans (5)
Sweet treat (5)
The Battle of the ---shed (3)
The animals lived by seven of these (12)
The cleverest of animals (4)
The dogs chased him off of the farm (8)
The hens had to give these up for sale (4)
The pigs drank this and ate the apples (4)
The pigs moved in there (5)
These keep animals in a particular pasture (6)
Thought (4)
Told stories about Sugarcandy Mountain (5)
Untruths (4)
Use of these was forbidden, not the use of beds (6)
Where the Seven Commandments were written (4)

Animal Farm Word Search 2 Answer Key

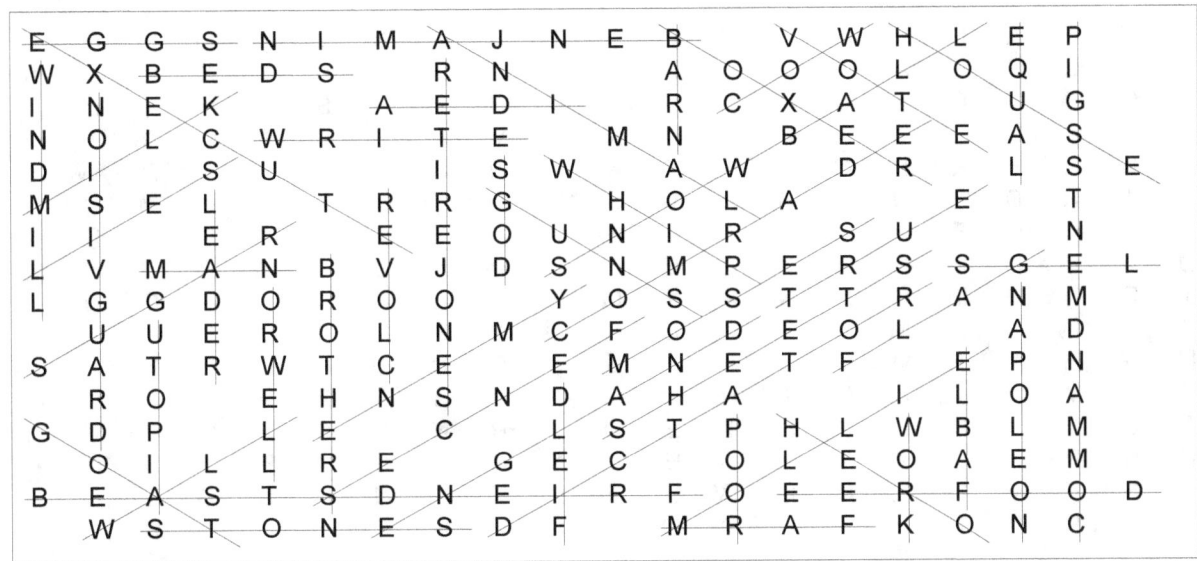

---- Farm (6)
----- of England (6)
A material symbol; the animals had a green & white one (4)
A perfect society (6)
A shortage of it triggered the revolution (4)
All animals are ----- (5)
All animals are equal; they are -------- (8)
All the habits of --- are evil. (3)
An individual casts one in an election (4)
Animal ---- (4)
Author (6)
Beasts of ---- (7)
Boxer and Benjamin, for example (7)
Boxer carried tons of these to make the windmill (6)
Donkey (8)
Duties; opposite of play (4)
Foe (5)
Four ---- good; two --- bad (4)
Horse who liked ribbons (6)
Huge, strong horse who had two maxims (5)
Job of the dogs (5)
Kill (7)
Liberated (4)
Means friend or fellow worker (7)
Men shot these at the animals (4)
Most animals learned to read and --- (5)
Motherly horse (6)
Napoleon's guard animals (4)
Not a lie; correct (4)
Not wealthy (4)

Old Major had one of these (6)
One in charge; Napoleon, for example (6)
One single ruler with total power (8)
Our Leader; the leader of the animals (8)
Owner of Manor Farm (5)
Pigs began to sleep in these (4)
Place of shelter for animals (4)
Place to plant crops (5)
Scape----- (4)
Snappy implement used to hit horses (4)
Snowball and Napoleon disagreed about building it (8)
Snowball was Animal ----, First Class (4)
Stop working after a period of time (6)
Story in which animals speak & act like humans (5)
Sweet treat (5)
The Battle of the ---shed (3)
The animals lived by seven of these (12)
The cleverest of animals (4)
The dogs chased him off of the farm (8)
The hens had to give these up for sale (4)
The pigs drank this and ate the apples (4)
The pigs moved in there (5)
These keep animals in a particular pasture (6)
Thought (4)
Told stories about Sugarcandy Mountain (5)
Untruths (4)
Use of these was forbidden, not the use of beds (6)
Where the Seven Commandments were written (4)

Animal Farm Word Search 3

```
R V W A L L F I E L D T B E N J A M I N
O Q O G O A T C D N S E L E R M O X O V
T Q D T Q S C L E M B B V D S M I F L L
A P P L E S K L I M A P V A E T L A T T
T S H E E P G A E F N I N S U I P R M W
C J R D H N M B U V S H R T L E C O M S
I F C C E K C W T I E W A O S F O O D F
D A P O L P L O O E F R V N C O W R G K
J R N N M O X N P R G E E E N I E A C D
S A W I B M V S I G R G N S N X L O M L
L G H M M W I E A J U B S D O F M E H F
E U Y W J A N T R J R A M B A R N U O W
A S M S H D L H T E O I R N A S G R V K
D B P F S Y R O W E L N S D G U E T S K
E N E M Y K R O W L E M E I N H S G E L
R W R I T E P F D O G S P S R E T I R E
```

ANIMAL	DICTATOR	GOAT	MILK	SYMBOL
APPLES	DOGS	GUARD	MOSES	TRUE
BARN	EGGS	GUNS	PIGS	UTOPIA
BEDS	ENEMY	HERO	POOR	VISION
BENJAMIN	ENGLAND	HOOF	POWER	VOTE
BOXER	FABLE	HOUSE	RAVEN	WALL
CLEVER	FARM	IDEA	RETIRE	WHIP
CLOVER	FIELD	JONES	REVOLUTION	WHYMPER
COMMITTEE	FLAG	LEADER	SHEEP	WINDMILL
COMRADE	FOOD	LEGS	SNOWBALL	WORK
COW	FREE	LIES	STONES	WRITE
DEBATE	FRIENDS	MAN	SUGAR	

Animal Farm Word Search 3 Answer Key

```
R V W A L L F I E L D   B E N J A M I N
O   O G O A T   D N   E E     O   O
T   T     C L A E M B B   D S   I F
A P P L E S K L I M A P V A E S T L A
T S H E E P G A E F N I   S T U I P R
C   R     N   B U V S H R T L E   O M
I F   C E     W T I E W A O S F O O D
D A   O L   L O O E F R N C O W R G
  R   N   M     N P R G E E   I E A C
  A W I B M V S I G R G N S N X L O  
L G H M M     A E A   U   S D O F M E H
E U Y       A N T R J R A M B A R N U O
A S M     D L H T E O I R   A S G R U
D   P     S     O W E L N   D G U E T S
E N E M Y K R O W L E     E I N H S G E L
R W R I T E P F D O G S P S R E T I R E
```

ANIMAL	DICTATOR	GOAT	MILK	SYMBOL
APPLES	DOGS	GUARD	MOSES	TRUE
BARN	EGGS	GUNS	PIGS	UTOPIA
BEDS	ENEMY	HERO	POOR	VISION
BENJAMIN	ENGLAND	HOOF	POWER	VOTE
BOXER	FABLE	HOUSE	RAVEN	WALL
CLEVER	FARM	IDEA	RETIRE	WHIP
CLOVER	FIELD	JONES	REVOLUTION	WHYMPER
COMMITTEE	FLAG	LEADER	SHEEP	WINDMILL
COMRADE	FOOD	LEGS	SNOWBALL	WORK
COW	FREE	LIES	STONES	WRITE
DEBATE	FRIENDS	MAN	SUGAR	

Animal Farm Word Search 4

```
A E T A B E D S U G A R A W H I S K E Y
P H W S E T Z H R A V E T N A O E F T Q G
P O V Z A I S E V F D T F L U L R S U F
L O S O T S H E P I J I L S B I O A F
E F T T S R W E P R O E R L O E I N L C
S M S M S E E E E L O E A X O F N E C
K I M A N C T P D U J R G M S D D S O
B L Q Y L U S X A T G K O N L H S M R X
O K B E C L G D E O C L O V E R R E S J
X K V E V I G R L P L W E G R A W P C L
E E X S D E E A F I B T E N D O B I O L
R E D O G S Q U E A L E R E P M Y H W Y
Z W M O E U W G L E R A F U N W O W L X
Y H A N X Z N L G F B M R F E E O S N V
R T O P I G S S B E N J A M I N M R E P
K J T A C T I C S A N I M A L T R Y K S
```

ANIMAL   DOGS   GOAT   MILK   STONES

APPLES   EGGS   GUARD   MOLLIE   SUGAR

BARN   ENEMY   GUNS   MOSES   TACTICS

BEASTS   EQUAL   HERO   PIGS   TRUE

BEDS   EXECUTE   HOOF   POOR   UTOPIA

BENJAMIN   FABLE   HOUSE   POWER   VOTE

BOXER   FARM   IDEA   RAVEN   WALL

CLEVER   FIELD   JONES   RETIRE   WHIP

CLOVER   FLAG   LEADER   SHEEP   WHISKEY

COMRADE   FOOD   LEGS   SHEETS   WHYMPER

COW   FREE   LIES   SNOWBALL   WORK

DEBATE   FRIENDS   MAN   SQUEALER   WRITE

Animal Farm Word Search 4 Answer Key

```
A  E  T  A  B  E  D  S  U  G  A  R  A  W  H  I  S  K  E  Y
P  H        E  T        H  R  A  V  E  N  A  O  E  F  S  Q
P  O  V     A     S        D  T  I  F  L  U  L  B  T  U
L  O     O  S  R  H  E  E  P  I  I  F  L  S  E  A  O  A
E     F  T     W  E  E  P  R  O  E  R  L  E  E  F  N  L
S  M        S  E  E  T  E  D  L  E  R  A  O  O  F  E     C
      I  M  A  N  C  T     D  U  T  R  G  M  S  D  S     O
B     L        L  U  S     A  T  O  N     O  N     S  M  R
O  K     B  E  C  L  G  D  E  O  C  L  O  V  E  R     E
X     V  E     I  G  R  A  L  P  L  W     N  A     W  P  C
E     E  X     D  E  E  R  A  F  I  B  T  E  D  O  A  I  O
R  E  D  O  G  S  Q  U  E  A  L  E  R  E  P  M  Y  H  W
      O  E  U     G  L  E  R  A  F  U  N  W  O  W
      A  N        N  L  G     B  M        E  E  O  S
T  O  P  I  G  S  S  B  E  N  J  A  M  I  N  M  R  E
J  T  A  C  T  I  C  S  A  N  I  M  A  L           Y  K  S
```

ANIMAL	DOGS	GOAT	MILK	STONES
APPLES	EGGS	GUARD	MOLLIE	SUGAR
BARN	ENEMY	GUNS	MOSES	TACTICS
BEASTS	EQUAL	HERO	PIGS	TRUE
BEDS	EXECUTE	HOOF	POOR	UTOPIA
BENJAMIN	FABLE	HOUSE	POWER	VOTE
BOXER	FARM	IDEA	RAVEN	WALL
CLEVER	FIELD	JONES	RETIRE	WHIP
CLOVER	FLAG	LEADER	SHEEP	WHISKEY
COMRADE	FOOD	LEGS	SHEETS	WHYMPER
COW	FREE	LIES	SNOWBALL	WORK
DEBATE	FRIENDS	MAN	SQUEALER	WRITE

Animal Farm Crossword 1

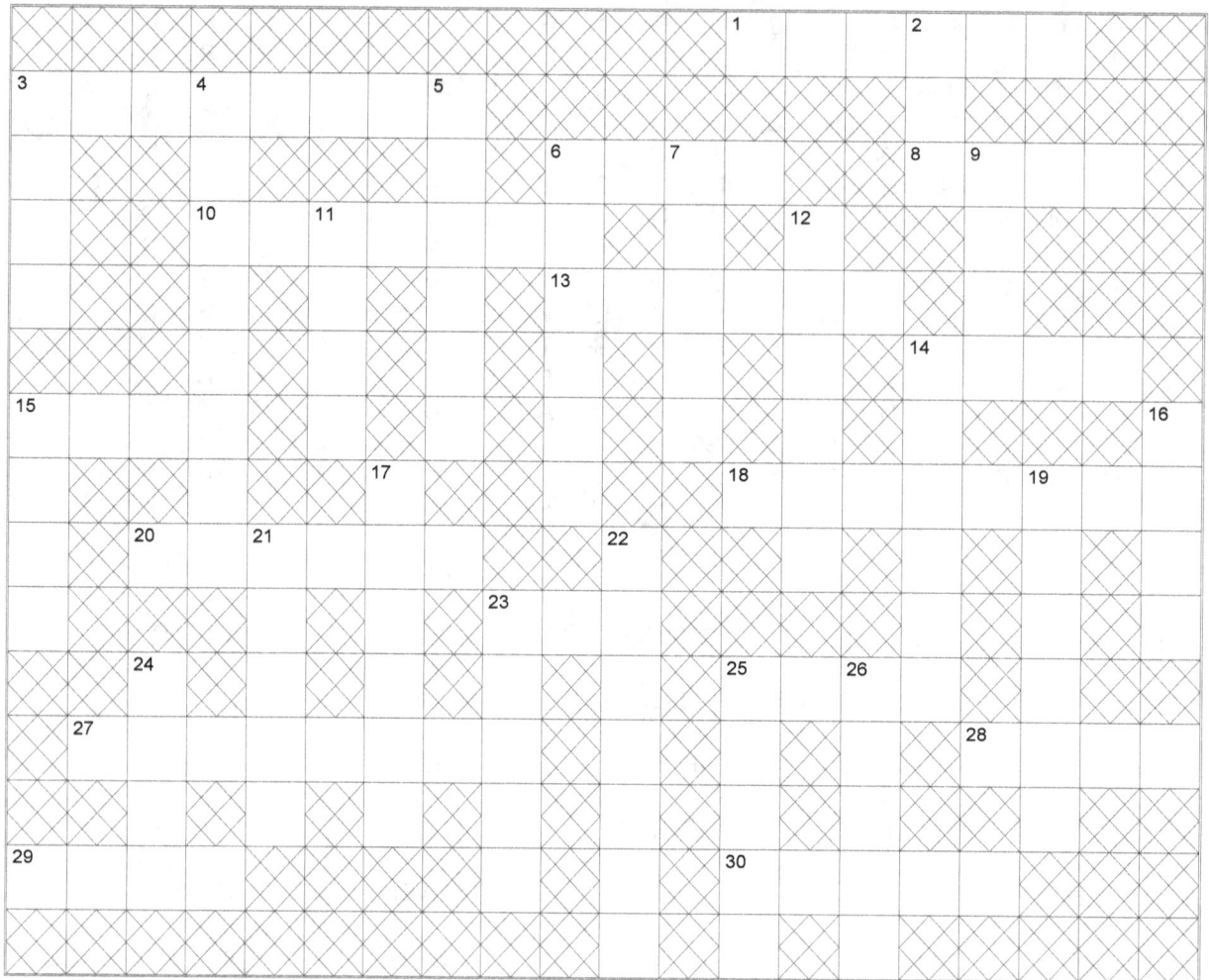

Across
1. These keep animals in a particular pasture
3. Snowball and Napoleon disagreed about building it
6. Napoleon's guard animals
8. Snappy implement used to hit horses
10. Means friend or fellow worker
13. ----- of England
14. An individual casts one in an election
15. Scape-----
18. Win to another point of view
20. Author
23. All the habits of --- are evil.
25. Place of shelter for animals
27. All animals are equal; they are --------
28. Animal ----
29. Untruths
30. Foe
Down
2. The Battle of the ---shed
3. Where the Seven Commandments were written
4. One single ruler with total power
5. One in charge; Napoleon, for example
6. Argument with rules
7. Job of the dogs
9. Snowball was Animal ----, First Class
11. The pigs drank this and ate the apples
12. Boxer carried tons of these to make the windmill
14. Old Major had one of these
15. Men shot these at the animals
16. Pigs began to sleep in these
17. Smart; astute
19. ---- Farm
21. Most animals learned to read and ---
22. Beasts of ----
23. Told stories about Sugarcandy Mountain
24. Not a lie; correct
25. Huge, strong horse who had two maxims
26. Moses was one

Animal Farm Crossword 1 Answer Key

Across
1. These keep animals in a particular pasture
3. Snowball and Napoleon disagreed about building it
6. Napoleon's guard animals
8. Snappy implement used to hit horses
10. Means friend or fellow worker
13. ----- of England
14. An individual casts one in an election
15. Scape-----
18. Win to another point of view
20. Author
23. All the habits of --- are evil.
25. Place of shelter for animals
27. All animals are equal; they are --------
28. Animal ----
29. Untruths
30. Foe

Down
2. The Battle of the ---shed
3. Where the Seven Commandments were written
4. One single ruler with total power
5. One in charge; Napoleon, for example
6. Argument with rules
7. Job of the dogs
9. Snowball was Animal ----, First Class
11. The pigs drank this and ate the apples
12. Boxer carried tons of these to make the windmill
14. Old Major had one of these
15. Men shot these at the animals
16. Pigs began to sleep in these
17. Smart; astute
19. ---- Farm
21. Most animals learned to read and ---
22. Beasts of ----
23. Told stories about Sugarcandy Mountain
24. Not a lie; correct
25. Huge, strong horse who had two maxims
26. Moses was one

Animal Farm Crossword 2

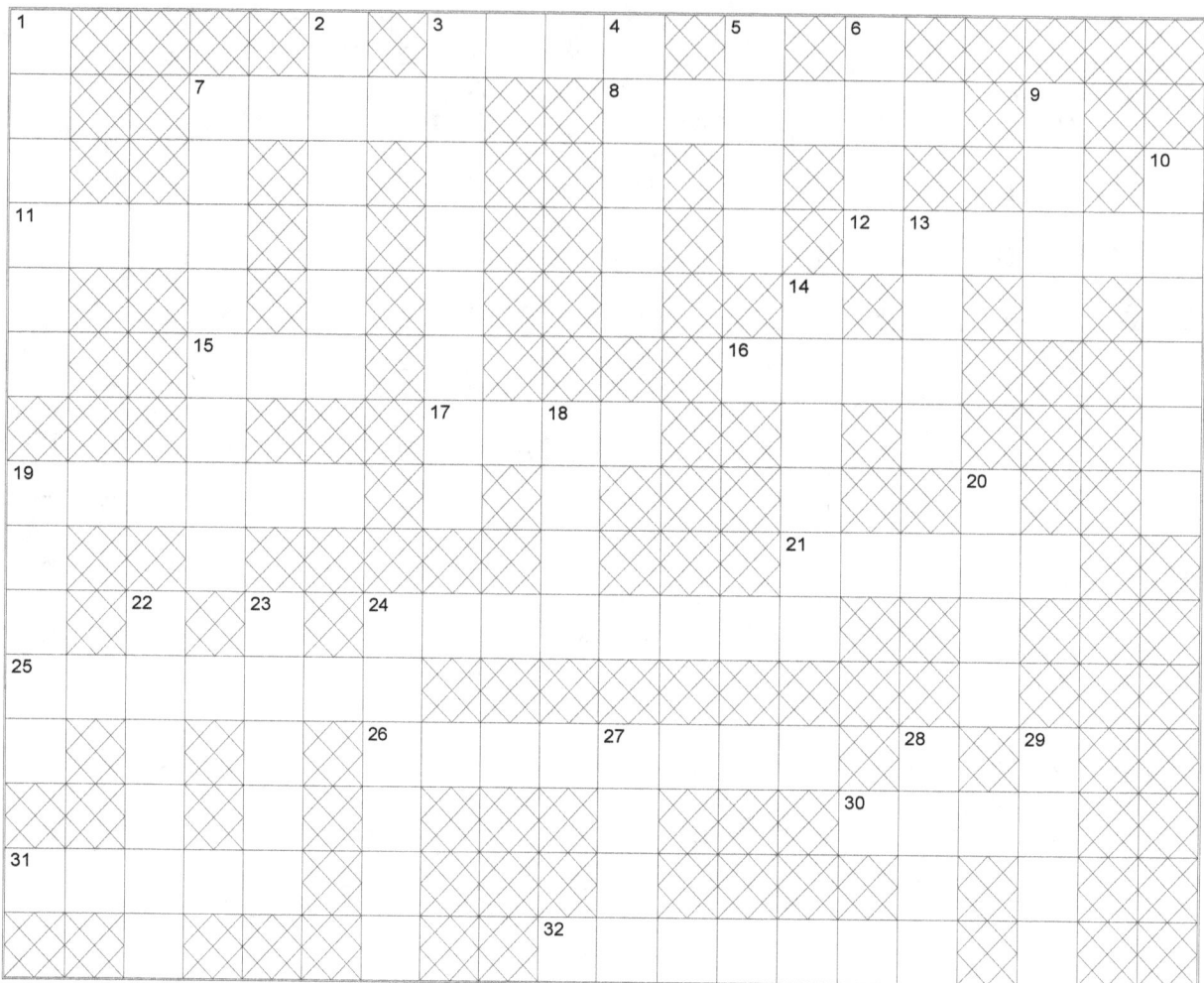

Across
- 3. Not wealthy
- 7. Most animals learned to read and ---
- 8. ---- Farm
- 11. Place of shelter for animals
- 12. One in charge; Napoleon, for example
- 15. All the habits of --- are evil.
- 16. A material symbol; the animals had a green & white one
- 17. Napoleon's guard animals
- 19. Horse who liked ribbons
- 21. All animals are -----
- 24. One single ruler with total power
- 25. Kill
- 26. All animals are equal; they are --------
- 30. Liberated
- 31. Place to plant crops
- 32. Means friend or fellow worker

Down
- 1. A sign; something that represents something else
- 2. Old Major had one of these
- 3. Win to another point of view
- 4. Moses was one
- 5. The pigs drank this and ate the apples
- 6. Where the Seven Commandments were written
- 7. Snowball and Napoleon disagreed about building it
- 9. Pigs began to sleep in these
- 10. Author
- 13. The hens had to give these up for sale
- 14. Smart; astute
- 18. Scape-----
- 19. Told stories about Sugarcandy Mountain
- 20. Animal ----
- 22. These keep animals in a particular pasture
- 23. Job of the dogs
- 24. Argument with rules
- 27. Snowball was Animal ----, First Class
- 28. Not a lie; correct
- 29. Four ---- good; two --- bad

Animal Farm Crossword 2 Answer Key

Across
- 3. Not wealthy
- 7. Most animals learned to read and ---
- 8. ---- Farm
- 11. Place of shelter for animals
- 12. One in charge; Napoleon, for example
- 15. All the habits of --- are evil.
- 16. A material symbol; the animals had a green & white one
- 17. Napoleon's guard animals
- 19. Horse who liked ribbons
- 21. All animals are -----
- 24. One single ruler with total power
- 25. Kill
- 26. All animals are equal; they are --------
- 30. Liberated
- 31. Place to plant crops
- 32. Means friend or fellow worker

Down
- 1. A sign; something that represents something else
- 2. Old Major had one of these
- 3. Win to another point of view
- 4. Moses was one
- 5. The pigs drank this and ate the apples
- 6. Where the Seven Commandments were written
- 7. Snowball and Napoleon disagreed about building it
- 9. Pigs began to sleep in these
- 10. Author
- 13. The hens had to give these up for sale
- 14. Smart; astute
- 18. Scape-----
- 19. Told stories about Sugarcandy Mountain
- 20. Animal ----
- 22. These keep animals in a particular pasture
- 23. Job of the dogs
- 24. Argument with rules
- 27. Snowball was Animal ----, First Class
- 28. Not a lie; correct
- 29. Four ---- good; two --- bad

Animal Farm Crossword 3

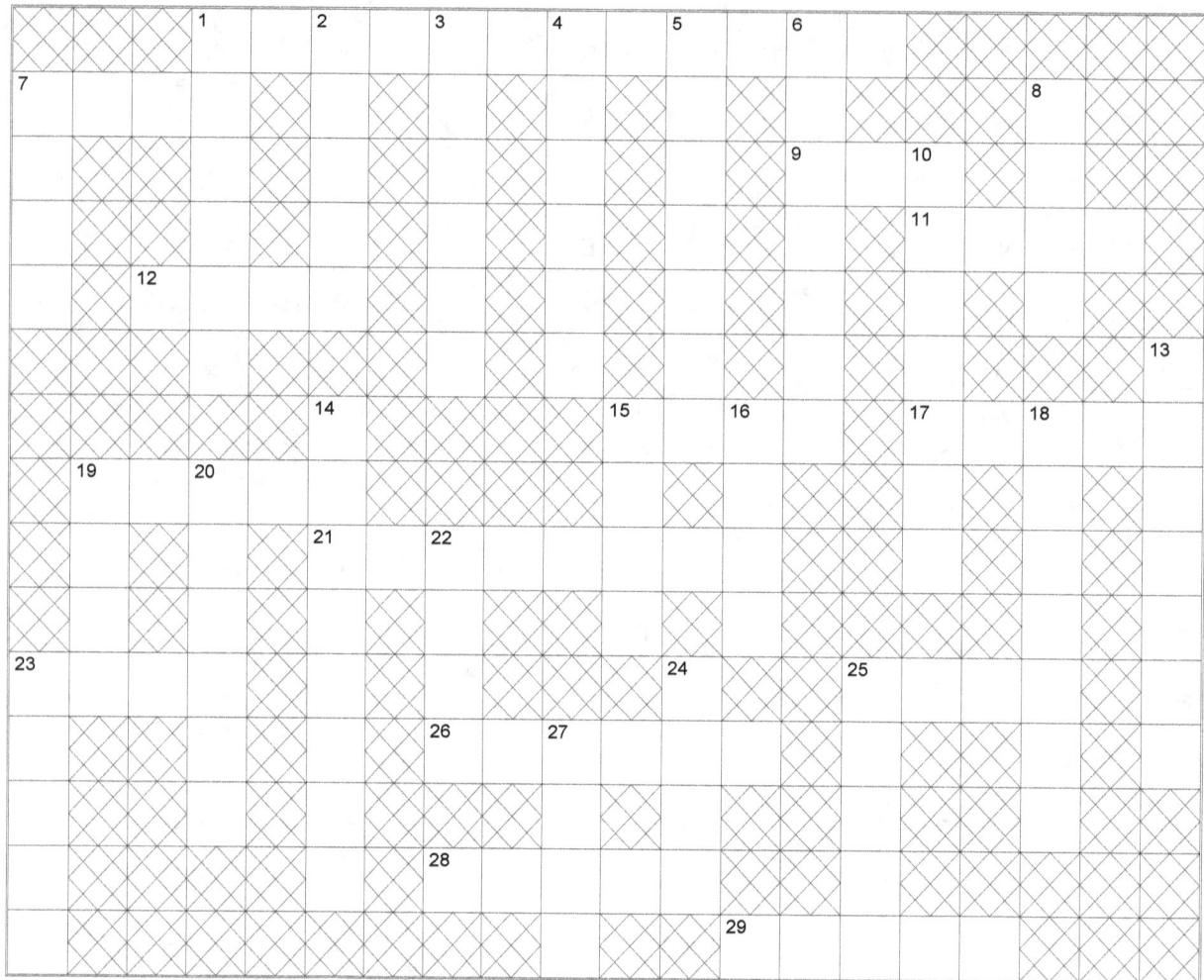

Across
1. The animals lived by seven of these
7. Where the Seven Commandments were written
9. The Battle of the ---shed
11. Snowball was Animal ----, First Class
12. Pigs began to sleep in these
15. Four ---- good; two --- bad
17. Influence; strength
19. Story in which animals speak & act like humans
21. Our Leader; the leader of the animals
23. The hens had to give these up for sale
25. Duties; opposite of play
26. Stop working after a period of time
28. The pigs moved in there
29. The wooly animals

Down
1. Smart; astute
2. Told stories about Sugarcandy Mountain
3. ---- Farm
4. Argument with rules
5. Kill
6. Strategies
7. Snappy implement used to hit horses
8. Place of shelter for animals
10. Middleman between Animal Farm & human world
13. Boxer and Benjamin, for example
14. Donkey
15. Untruths
16. Men shot these at the animals
18. The pigs found a case of this and drank too much
19. A material symbol; the animals had a green & white one
20. ----- of England
22. Not wealthy
23. All animals are -----
24. Liberated
25. Most animals learned to read and ---
27. Not a lie; correct

42
Copyrighted

Animal Farm Crossword 3 Answer Key

Across
1. The animals lived by seven of these
7. Where the Seven Commandments were written
9. The Battle of the ---shed
11. Snowball was Animal ----, First Class
12. Pigs began to sleep in these
15. Four ---- good; two --- bad
17. Influence; strength
19. Story in which animals speak & act like humans
21. Our Leader; the leader of the animals
23. The hens had to give these up for sale
25. Duties; opposite of play
26. Stop working after a period of time
28. The pigs moved in there
29. The wooly animals

Down
1. Smart; astute
2. Told stories about Sugarcandy Mountain
3. ---- Farm
4. Argument with rules
5. Kill
6. Strategies
7. Snappy implement used to hit horses
8. Place of shelter for animals
10. Middleman between Animal Farm & human world
13. Boxer and Benjamin, for example
14. Donkey
15. Untruths
16. Men shot these at the animals
18. The pigs found a case of this and drank too much
19. A material symbol; the animals had a green & white one
20. ----- of England
22. Not wealthy
23. All animals are -----
24. Liberated
25. Most animals learned to read and ---
27. Not a lie; correct

Animal Farm Crossword 4

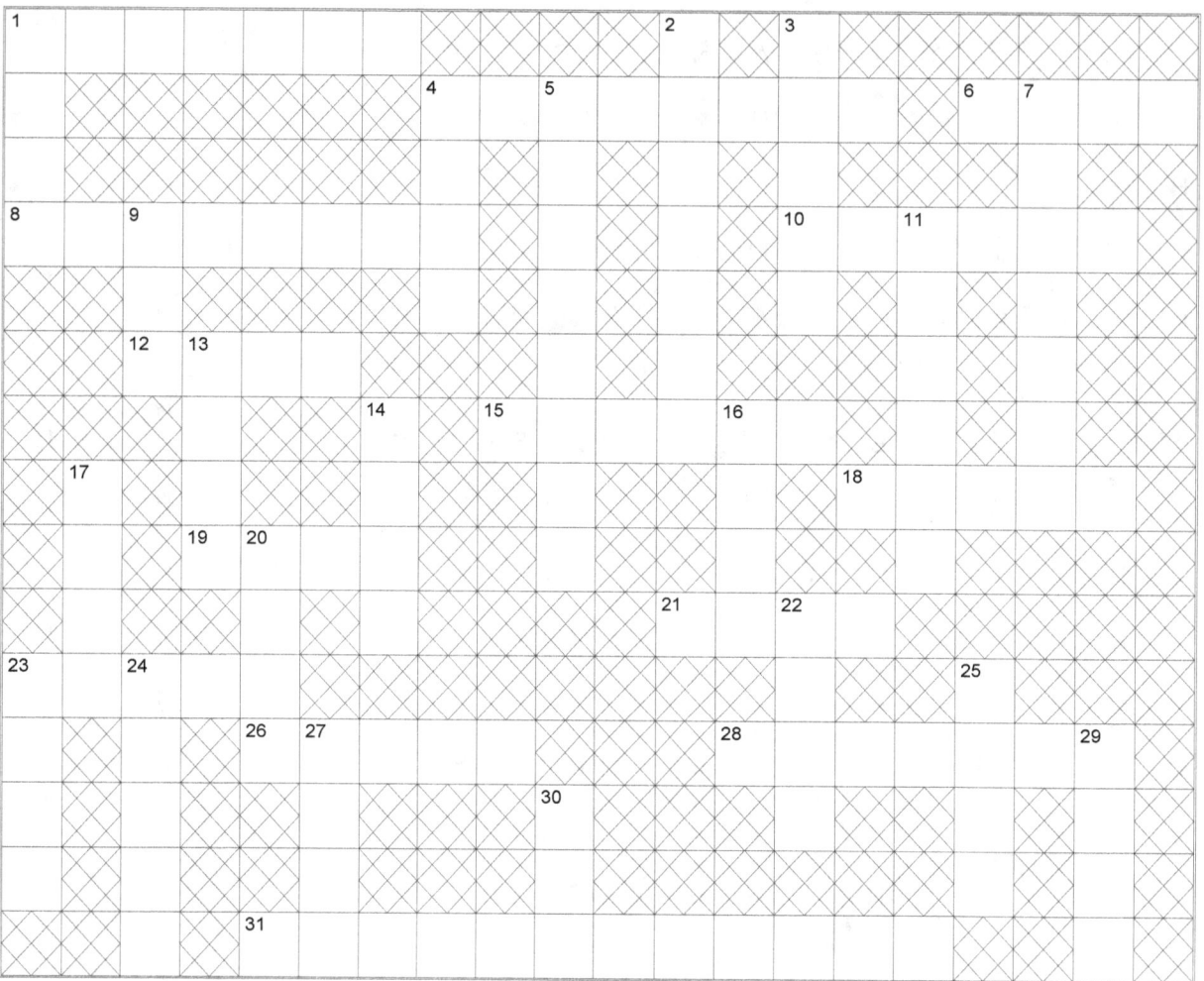

Across
1. Boxer and Benjamin, for example
4. Donkey
6. Pigs began to sleep in these
8. One single ruler with total power
10. One in charge; Napoleon, for example
12. Snappy implement used to hit horses
15. ----- of England
18. Moses was one
19. A material symbol; the animals had a green & white one
21. Four ---- good; two --- bad
23. Story in which animals speak & act like humans
26. The wooly animals
28. Beasts of ----
31. The animals lived by seven of these

Down
1. A shortage of it triggered the revolution
2. Strategies
3. Place to plant crops
4. Place of shelter for animals
5. Our Leader; the leader of the animals
7. Kill
9. The Battle of the ---shed
11. ---- Farm
13. Boxer split his; also the flag had one on it
14. The cleverest of animals
16. Not a lie; correct
17. Thought
20. Untruths
22. Men shot these at the animals
23. Animal ----
24. Huge, strong horse who had two maxims
25. Where the Seven Commandments were written
27. Snowball was Animal ----, First Class
29. Napoleon's guard animals
30. All the habits of --- are evil.

Animal Farm Crossword 4 Answer Key

	1 F	R	I	E	N	D	S			2 T		3 F			
	O						4 B	E	5 N	J	A	M	I	N	6 B	7 E	D	S
	O						A		A		C		E			X		
8 D	I	9 C	T	A	T	O	R		P		T		10 L	11 E	A	D	E	R
		O					N		O		I		D		N		C	
		12 W	13 H	I	P				L		C				I		U	
			O			14 P	15 B	E	A	S	T	S		16 T		M		T
	17 I		O			I			O		R			18 R	A	V	E	N
	D		19 F	20 L	A	G			N		U			L				
	E			I					21 L	E	22 G	S						
23 F	A	24 B	L	E							U			25 W				
A		O		26 S	27 H	E	E	P		28 E	N	G	L	A	N	29 D		
R		X			E				30 M		S			L		O		
M		E			R				A					L		G		
		R		31 C	O	M	M	A	N	D	M	E	N	T	S			
															S			

Across
1. Boxer and Benjamin, for example
4. Donkey
6. Pigs began to sleep in these
8. One single ruler with total power
10. One in charge; Napoleon, for example
12. Snappy implement used to hit horses
15. ----- of England
18. Moses was one
19. A material symbol; the animals had a green & white one
21. Four ---- good; two --- bad
23. Story in which animals speak & act like humans
26. The wooly animals
28. Beasts of ----
31. The animals lived by seven of these

Down
1. A shortage of it triggered the revolution
2. Strategies
3. Place to plant crops
4. Place of shelter for animals
5. Our Leader; the leader of the animals
7. Kill
9. The Battle of the ---shed
11. ---- Farm
13. Boxer split his; also the flag had one on it
14. The cleverest of animals
16. Not a lie; correct
17. Thought
20. Untruths
22. Men shot these at the animals
23. Animal ----
24. Huge, strong horse who had two maxims
25. Where the Seven Commandments were written
27. Snowball was Animal ----, First Class
29. Napoleon's guard animals
30. All the habits of --- are evil.

Animal Farm

RETIRE	VOTE	FREDERICK	FLAG	EQUAL
GUARD	DEBATE	GOAT	SUGAR	RAVEN
IDEA	MAN	FREE SPACE	NAPOLEON	FABLE
WHYMPER	CLOVER	SNOWBALL	APPLES	TACTICS
VISION	WORK	FRIENDS	BARN	DICTATOR

Animal Farm

LEADER	GUNS	ORWELL	UTOPIA	BROTHERS
POOR	LEGS	STONES	COW	COMRADE
FOOD	HOUSE	FREE SPACE	SHEEP	MOLLIE
EGGS	SHEETS	HOOF	WALL	MOSES
OLD	SQUEALER	MILK	WINDMILL	WHIP

Animal Farm

PIGS	WRITE	WHYMPER	REVOLUTION	GUNS
SYMBOL	FREDERICK	BEASTS	LEADER	BROTHERS
EQUAL	CLEVER	FREE SPACE	BOXER	TRUE
DEBATE	TACTICS	COMMANDMENTS	ENGLAND	LEGS
WHIP	HOOF	PERSUADE	GUARD	RETIRE

Animal Farm

JONES	ANIMAL	EGGS	RAVEN	LIES
SQUEALER	WALL	FREE	FRIENDS	VOTE
BARN	ORWELL	FREE SPACE	CLOVER	BEDS
VISION	MAN	FIELD	POWER	MOLLIE
STONES	HERO	FENCES	DICTATOR	FOOD

Animal Farm

BOXER	CLOVER	FOOD	GUNS	COMRADE
EXECUTE	ORWELL	LIES	RETIRE	BENJAMIN
WALL	MOLLIE	FREE SPACE	ENGLAND	FREDERICK
SHEETS	FARM	WINDMILL	VISION	FENCES
ANIMAL	RAVEN	JONES	IDEA	TACTICS

Animal Farm

PIGS	FIELD	PERSUADE	POWER	LEGS
COMMANDMENTS	ENEMY	GUARD	SUGAR	UTOPIA
OLD	WHYMPER	FREE SPACE	HOUSE	HERO
FREE	SYMBOL	MAN	MILK	WORK
EQUAL	VOTE	CLEVER	SNOWBALL	POOR

Animal Farm

IDEA	MILK	WHIP	NAPOLEON	DICTATOR
COMMANDMENTS	JONES	SYMBOL	BENJAMIN	FABLE
MOSES	CLOVER	FREE SPACE	POWER	VISION
BARN	WORK	HOUSE	SHEETS	FRIENDS
POOR	LEADER	LIES	ORWELL	ENGLAND

Animal Farm

ENEMY	SQUEALER	FENCES	EXECUTE	PIGS
WHISKEY	EQUAL	GUARD	FLAG	BOXER
WRITE	VOTE	FREE SPACE	OLD	REVOLUTION
RAVEN	BEASTS	DOGS	STONES	EGGS
UTOPIA	TRUE	CLEVER	BROTHERS	FOOD

Animal Farm

TACTICS	LIES	REVOLUTION	ANIMAL	FENCES
APPLES	MAN	BEASTS	COMMITTEE	VOTE
CLEVER	JONES	FREE SPACE	HERO	TRUE
BROTHERS	FREE	HOOF	MOLLIE	RAVEN
BATTLE	PERSUADE	WHIP	NAPOLEON	ORWELL

Animal Farm

DEBATE	EXECUTE	BENJAMIN	CLOVER	SYMBOL
FABLE	WHISKEY	SHEETS	IDEA	WRITE
COW	FARM	FREE SPACE	BARN	BOXER
VISION	WHYMPER	POWER	PIGS	COMRADE
COMMANDMENTS	DICTATOR	FLAG	OLD	ENGLAND

Animal Farm

LEGS	FENCES	EQUAL	VISION	POWER
UTOPIA	PIGS	BATTLE	SUGAR	ENGLAND
APPLES	BOXER	FREE SPACE	DOGS	MOSES
FLAG	WHIP	FRIENDS	HOOF	ORWELL
JONES	BEDS	SYMBOL	SHEEP	SNOWBALL

Animal Farm

COMMITTEE	BEASTS	DEBATE	WORK	FREE
GUNS	EGGS	ANIMAL	ENEMY	COMRADE
BENJAMIN	FABLE	FREE SPACE	VOTE	TACTICS
SHEETS	NAPOLEON	TRUE	BARN	LEADER
RAVEN	POOR	STONES	RETIRE	FIELD

Animal Farm

SYMBOL	BEDS	ORWELL	FARM	FENCES
SHEEP	CLEVER	OLD	APPLES	ANIMAL
TRUE	HOOF	FREE SPACE	IDEA	MILK
VISION	FIELD	PERSUADE	SNOWBALL	WHIP
JONES	COMMANDMENTS	LEGS	COMMITTEE	FREE

Animal Farm

FABLE	BATTLE	BENJAMIN	DOGS	EGGS
STONES	GOAT	PIGS	FRIENDS	LIES
GUARD	FREDERICK	FREE SPACE	DEBATE	MOSES
ENEMY	BOXER	RETIRE	VOTE	HOUSE
DICTATOR	LEADER	WORK	BROTHERS	WHYMPER

Animal Farm

BARN	PERSUADE	WALL	FOOD	COMMITTEE
FIELD	HERO	MAN	JONES	BEDS
FREDERICK	POWER	FREE SPACE	MOLLIE	NAPOLEON
FLAG	FREE	WRITE	CLOVER	PIGS
ENGLAND	GUNS	ANIMAL	REVOLUTION	HOOF

Animal Farm

FABLE	COMRADE	FENCES	SUGAR	EQUAL
SYMBOL	DOGS	EXECUTE	BEASTS	EGGS
POOR	UTOPIA	FREE SPACE	FARM	FRIENDS
OLD	LIES	ENEMY	VISION	GUARD
BATTLE	CLEVER	SNOWBALL	MOSES	BOXER

Animal Farm

ORWELL	POWER	BARN	REVOLUTION	WRITE
BATTLE	JONES	WORK	RETIRE	BEASTS
SHEEP	GOAT	FREE SPACE	SQUEALER	MILK
OLD	CLOVER	VOTE	PERSUADE	DOGS
FRIENDS	COMMITTEE	LIES	BEDS	LEGS

Animal Farm

SUGAR	HOUSE	DICTATOR	WALL	BOXER
TACTICS	POOR	COW	WHIP	EGGS
RAVEN	HERO	FREE SPACE	IDEA	GUNS
ANIMAL	CLEVER	PIGS	FLAG	FIELD
APPLES	FENCES	DEBATE	WHISKEY	MOSES

Animal Farm

COMMITTEE	HOUSE	NAPOLEON	FABLE	POOR
BARN	BATTLE	IDEA	EQUAL	PIGS
APPLES	MOSES	FREE SPACE	BOXER	POWER
HERO	WRITE	WALL	MAN	LIES
SHEETS	GOAT	VOTE	RAVEN	CLOVER

Animal Farm

FENCES	DICTATOR	JONES	WHIP	MOLLIE
COMMANDMENTS	FRIENDS	SUGAR	CLEVER	FOOD
COMRADE	TACTICS	FREE SPACE	FARM	WINDMILL
LEGS	OLD	BEASTS	MILK	BROTHERS
SYMBOL	WHISKEY	DOGS	DEBATE	REVOLUTION

Animal Farm

FREDERICK	WRITE	FRIENDS	SYMBOL	WALL
IDEA	MOSES	MILK	WHYMPER	FENCES
APPLES	BEDS	FREE SPACE	WINDMILL	REVOLUTION
GOAT	HERO	MAN	WORK	COMRADE
DOGS	HOOF	FOOD	POWER	LIES

Animal Farm

BEASTS	GUARD	WHISKEY	COMMITTEE	SHEETS
RETIRE	PIGS	FLAG	GUNS	JONES
BATTLE	SUGAR	FREE SPACE	SNOWBALL	TACTICS
SHEEP	FREE	ORWELL	FIELD	EXECUTE
NAPOLEON	FABLE	TRUE	PERSUADE	BROTHERS

Animal Farm

SHEETS	SNOWBALL	BOXER	FREE	LEGS
JONES	WHYMPER	SHEEP	MOLLIE	COMMITTEE
WRITE	APPLES	FREE SPACE	BARN	EXECUTE
WHISKEY	COMMANDMENTS	BEASTS	FARM	TRUE
RETIRE	SYMBOL	FABLE	FLAG	WALL

Animal Farm

GUARD	IDEA	CLOVER	ANIMAL	COW
UTOPIA	BATTLE	LIES	EGGS	SUGAR
ENGLAND	PIGS	FREE SPACE	COMRADE	MILK
POWER	BEDS	GOAT	BENJAMIN	DICTATOR
FOOD	NAPOLEON	WINDMILL	ORWELL	WORK

Animal Farm

COW	TRUE	SYMBOL	BENJAMIN	CLOVER
ORWELL	BROTHERS	DOGS	COMMANDMENTS	WALL
MOLLIE	BEDS	FREE SPACE	BOXER	SHEEP
COMMITTEE	EGGS	SQUEALER	GUARD	EQUAL
WRITE	APPLES	FREE	RETIRE	SHEETS

Animal Farm

JONES	FLAG	HOOF	WINDMILL	WHISKEY
STONES	ENGLAND	BATTLE	WHYMPER	FOOD
VOTE	COMRADE	FREE SPACE	POOR	IDEA
FIELD	DICTATOR	BEASTS	SNOWBALL	LEGS
MAN	GOAT	LEADER	OLD	UTOPIA

Animal Farm

VISION	LEADER	RAVEN	EGGS	IDEA
CLEVER	SNOWBALL	HERO	REVOLUTION	BROTHERS
WINDMILL	HOUSE	FREE SPACE	FABLE	NAPOLEON
SHEETS	BEASTS	EQUAL	GOAT	FRIENDS
MOLLIE	ORWELL	DOGS	FREE	SHEEP

Animal Farm

FENCES	LEGS	UTOPIA	SQUEALER	SYMBOL
ANIMAL	FOOD	PERSUADE	BENJAMIN	BATTLE
CLOVER	RETIRE	FREE SPACE	HOOF	FLAG
WORK	APPLES	STONES	BOXER	ENGLAND
MOSES	FIELD	COMRADE	FARM	WALL

Animal Farm

FRIENDS	COMMITTEE	WORK	WRITE	FLAG
FREE	BATTLE	TACTICS	SHEETS	RAVEN
TRUE	EGGS	FREE SPACE	IDEA	BEDS
BENJAMIN	FOOD	REVOLUTION	BARN	GUARD
MILK	SQUEALER	PERSUADE	BOXER	EXECUTE

Animal Farm

WHYMPER	VISION	ENGLAND	WHISKEY	SNOWBALL
APPLES	SYMBOL	DICTATOR	EQUAL	UTOPIA
HOUSE	OLD	FREE SPACE	FABLE	LEADER
COW	BROTHERS	ANIMAL	MAN	ENEMY
LIES	RETIRE	WHIP	ORWELL	HOOF

Animal Farm

RAVEN	COMRADE	REVOLUTION	LEADER	GUARD
HOUSE	FLAG	COMMANDMENTS	PIGS	PERSUADE
SHEETS	BENJAMIN	FREE SPACE	APPLES	TACTICS
SUGAR	SQUEALER	RETIRE	WINDMILL	BARN
BOXER	FRIENDS	BEASTS	OLD	LIES

Animal Farm

HOOF	NAPOLEON	STONES	WALL	MAN
ENGLAND	EQUAL	ENEMY	VOTE	VISION
WORK	BEDS	FREE SPACE	FENCES	ORWELL
SYMBOL	FREE	UTOPIA	SNOWBALL	BATTLE
COMMITTEE	ANIMAL	CLEVER	JONES	FABLE

Animal Farm Vocabulary Word List

No.	Word	Clue/Definition
1.	APATHY	Lack of interest or emotion
2.	CAPITULATED	Gave up all resistance
3.	CONCILIATORY	Showing good-will; peace-making
4.	CONTEMPTUOUSLY	Scornfully
5.	CONTROVERSIES	Disputes
6.	COUNTENANCE	Facial expression
7.	CRUCIAL	Critical; of supreme importance
8.	CYNICAL	Bitterly mocking
9.	EMBOLDENED	Encouraged; made brave; gave courage to
10.	FALTER	Waver in confidence; hesitate; fail
11.	FILIAL	Befitting a son or daughter
12.	IGNOMINIOUS	Disgraceful; shameful
13.	IMPENDING	About to take place
14.	IMPROMPTU	Not rehearsed; on the spur of the moment
15.	INDEFATIGABLE	Untiring; tireless
16.	INEBRIATES	Drunkards
17.	IRREPRESSIBLE	Impossible to control or restrain
18.	LURKING	Exist concealed or unsuspected
19.	OBSTINATE	Stubbornly inflexible
20.	PENSION	Sum of money paid as a retirement benefit
21.	PERPETUALLY	Continually
22.	POSTHUMOUSLY	After one's death
23.	PREEMINENT	Outstanding
24.	PRETEXT	Excuse
25.	RETINUE	Those accompanying a person of rank
26.	SHREWD	Astute; clever
27.	SIMULTANEOUSLY	Happening at the same time
28.	SOLEMNLY	Seriously; deeply earnest
29.	SUPERANNUATED	Retired because of age or infirmity
30.	TUMULT	Commotion
31.	TYRANNY	Absolute power; esp. when used unjustly or cruelly
32.	UNANIMOUSLY	In complete agreement
33.	VIVACIOUS	Lively; spirited

Animal Farm Vocabulary Fill In The Blank 1

_____ 1. Lively; spirited

_____ 2. Impossible to control or restrain

_____ 3. Retired because of age or infirmity

_____ 4. Excuse

_____ 5. Waver in confidence; hesitate; fail

_____ 6. Critical; of supreme importance

_____ 7. In complete agreement

_____ 8. Absolute power; esp. when used unjustly or cruelly

_____ 9. Scornfully

_____ 10. Showing good-will; peace-making

_____ 11. Facial expression

_____ 12. Continually

_____ 13. Not rehearsed; on the spur of the moment

_____ 14. Disgraceful; shameful

_____ 15. Encouraged; made brave; gave courage to

_____ 16. After one's death

_____ 17. Stubbornly inflexible

_____ 18. Astute; clever

_____ 19. Gave up all resistance

_____ 20. Sum of money paid as a retirement benefit

Animal Farm Vocabulary Fill In The Blank 1 Answer Key

VIVACIOUS	1. Lively; spirited
IRREPRESSIBLE	2. Impossible to control or restrain
SUPERANNUATED	3. Retired because of age or infirmity
PRETEXT	4. Excuse
FALTER	5. Waver in confidence; hesitate; fail
CRUCIAL	6. Critical; of supreme importance
UNANIMOUSLY	7. In complete agreement
TYRANNY	8. Absolute power; esp. when used unjustly or cruelly
CONTEMPTUOUSLY	9. Scornfully
CONCILIATORY	10. Showing good-will; peace-making
COUNTENANCE	11. Facial expression
PERPETUALLY	12. Continually
IMPROMPTU	13. Not rehearsed; on the spur of the moment
IGNOMINIOUS	14. Disgraceful; shameful
EMBOLDENED	15. Encouraged; made brave; gave courage to
POSTHUMOUSLY	16. After one's death
OBSTINATE	17. Stubbornly inflexible
SHREWD	18. Astute; clever
CAPITULATED	19. Gave up all resistance
PENSION	20. Sum of money paid as a retirement benefit

Animal Farm Vocabulary Fill In The Blank 2

_____ 1. Stubbornly inflexible

_____ 2. Seriously; deeply earnest

_____ 3. Happening at the same time

_____ 4. Disputes

_____ 5. Commotion

_____ 6. After one's death

_____ 7. Excuse

_____ 8. Facial expression

_____ 9. Retired because of age or infirmity

_____ 10. Critical; of supreme importance

_____ 11. Continually

_____ 12. Exist concealed or unsuspected

_____ 13. About to take place

_____ 14. Drunkards

_____ 15. In complete agreement

_____ 16. Scornfully

_____ 17. Gave up all resistance

_____ 18. Outstanding

_____ 19. Befitting a son or daughter

_____ 20. Encouraged; made brave; gave courage to

Animal Farm Vocabulary Fill In The Blank 2 Answer Key

OBSTINATE	1. Stubbornly inflexible
SOLEMNLY	2. Seriously; deeply earnest
SIMULTANEOUSLY	3. Happening at the same time
CONTROVERSIES	4. Disputes
TUMULT	5. Commotion
POSTHUMOUSLY	6. After one's death
PRETEXT	7. Excuse
COUNTENANCE	8. Facial expression
SUPERANNUATED	9. Retired because of age or infirmity
CRUCIAL	10. Critical; of supreme importance
PERPETUALLY	11. Continually
LURKING	12. Exist concealed or unsuspected
IMPENDING	13. About to take place
INEBRIATES	14. Drunkards
UNANIMOUSLY	15. In complete agreement
CONTEMPTUOUSLY	16. Scornfully
CAPITULATED	17. Gave up all resistance
PREEMINENT	18. Outstanding
FILIAL	19. Befitting a son or daughter
EMBOLDENED	20. Encouraged; made brave; gave courage to

Animal Farm Vocabulary Fill In The Blank 3

_____ 1. After one's death

_____ 2. Lack of interest or emotion

_____ 3. Retired because of age or infirmity

_____ 4. Showing good-will; peace-making

_____ 5. Scornfully

_____ 6. Disgraceful; shameful

_____ 7. Continually

_____ 8. Stubbornly inflexible

_____ 9. Happening at the same time

_____ 10. Befitting a son or daughter

_____ 11. Bitterly mocking

_____ 12. Not rehearsed; on the spur of the moment

_____ 13. Sum of money paid as a retirement benefit

_____ 14. Seriously; deeply earnest

_____ 15. Those accompanying a person of rank

_____ 16. Impossible to control or restrain

_____ 17. Absolute power; esp. when used unjustly or cruelly

_____ 18. Encouraged; made brave; gave courage to

_____ 19. Lively; spirited

_____ 20. About to take place

Animal Farm Vocabulary Fill In The Blank 3 Answer Key

POSTHUMOUSLY	1. After one's death
APATHY	2. Lack of interest or emotion
SUPERANNUATED	3. Retired because of age or infirmity
CONCILIATORY	4. Showing good-will; peace-making
CONTEMPTUOUSLY	5. Scornfully
IGNOMINIOUS	6. Disgraceful; shameful
PERPETUALLY	7. Continually
OBSTINATE	8. Stubbornly inflexible
SIMULTANEOUSLY	9. Happening at the same time
FILIAL	10. Befitting a son or daughter
CYNICAL	11. Bitterly mocking
IMPROMPTU	12. Not rehearsed; on the spur of the moment
PENSION	13. Sum of money paid as a retirement benefit
SOLEMNLY	14. Seriously; deeply earnest
RETINUE	15. Those accompanying a person of rank
IRREPRESSIBLE	16. Impossible to control or restrain
TYRANNY	17. Absolute power; esp. when used unjustly or cruelly
EMBOLDENED	18. Encouraged; made brave; gave courage to
VIVACIOUS	19. Lively; spirited
IMPENDING	20. About to take place

Animal Farm Vocabulary Fill In The Blank 4

_____ 1. Continually

_____ 2. Those accompanying a person of rank

_____ 3. Bitterly mocking

_____ 4. Impossible to control or restrain

_____ 5. Outstanding

_____ 6. Befitting a son or daughter

_____ 7. Not rehearsed; on the spur of the moment

_____ 8. Disputes

_____ 9. Showing good-will; peace-making

_____ 10. In complete agreement

_____ 11. Happening at the same time

_____ 12. Encouraged; made brave; gave courage to

_____ 13. Lack of interest or emotion

_____ 14. Facial expression

_____ 15. After one's death

_____ 16. Disgraceful; shameful

_____ 17. Waver in confidence; hesitate; fail

_____ 18. Retired because of age or infirmity

_____ 19. About to take place

_____ 20. Commotion

Animal Farm Vocabulary Fill In The Blank 4 Answer Key

PERPETUALLY	1. Continually
RETINUE	2. Those accompanying a person of rank
CYNICAL	3. Bitterly mocking
IRREPRESSIBLE	4. Impossible to control or restrain
PREEMINENT	5. Outstanding
FILIAL	6. Befitting a son or daughter
IMPROMPTU	7. Not rehearsed; on the spur of the moment
CONTROVERSIES	8. Disputes
CONCILIATORY	9. Showing good-will; peace-making
UNANIMOUSLY	10. In complete agreement
SIMULTANEOUSLY	11. Happening at the same time
EMBOLDENED	12. Encouraged; made brave; gave courage to
APATHY	13. Lack of interest or emotion
COUNTENANCE	14. Facial expression
POSTHUMOUSLY	15. After one's death
IGNOMINIOUS	16. Disgraceful; shameful
FALTER	17. Waver in confidence; hesitate; fail
SUPERANNUATED	18. Retired because of age or infirmity
IMPENDING	19. About to take place
TUMULT	20. Commotion

Animal Farm Vocabulary Matching 1

___ 1. VIVACIOUS   A. Lively; spirited
___ 2. CONTROVERSIES   B. Facial expression
___ 3. IMPENDING   C. Encouraged; made brave; gave courage to
___ 4. COUNTENANCE   D. Retired because of age or infirmity
___ 5. CRUCIAL   E. Sum of money paid as a retirement benefit
___ 6. PRETEXT   F. Befitting a son or daughter
___ 7. SUPERANNUATED   G. About to take place
___ 8. OBSTINATE   H. Exist concealed or unsuspected
___ 9. SIMULTANEOUSLY   I. After one's death
___10. IMPROMPTU   J. Outstanding
___11. PENSION   K. Stubbornly inflexible
___12. CONCILIATORY   L. Bitterly mocking
___13. CONTEMPTUOUSLY   M. Waver in confidence; hesitate; fail
___14. CYNICAL   N. Those accompanying a person of rank
___15. LURKING   O. Showing good-will; peace-making
___16. FALTER   P. In complete agreement
___17. UNANIMOUSLY   Q. Excuse
___18. PREEMINENT   R. Scornfully
___19. FILIAL   S. Gave up all resistance
___20. CAPITULATED   T. Critical; of supreme importance
___21. TYRANNY   U. Not rehearsed; on the spur of the moment
___22. POSTHUMOUSLY   V. Absolute power; esp. when used unjustly or cruelly
___23. RETINUE   W. Disputes
___24. IGNOMINIOUS   X. Happening at the same time
___25. EMBOLDENED   Y. Disgraceful; shameful

Animal Farm Vocabulary Matching 1 Answer Key

A - 1. VIVACIOUS	A. Lively; spirited
W - 2. CONTROVERSIES	B. Facial expression
G - 3. IMPENDING	C. Encouraged; made brave; gave courage to
B - 4. COUNTENANCE	D. Retired because of age or infirmity
T - 5. CRUCIAL	E. Sum of money paid as a retirement benefit
Q - 6. PRETEXT	F. Befitting a son or daughter
D - 7. SUPERANNUATED	G. About to take place
K - 8. OBSTINATE	H. Exist concealed or unsuspected
X - 9. SIMULTANEOUSLY	I. After one's death
U - 10. IMPROMPTU	J. Outstanding
E - 11. PENSION	K. Stubbornly inflexible
O - 12. CONCILIATORY	L. Bitterly mocking
R - 13. CONTEMPTUOUSLY	M. Waver in confidence; hesitate; fail
L - 14. CYNICAL	N. Those accompanying a person of rank
H - 15. LURKING	O. Showing good-will; peace-making
M - 16. FALTER	P. In complete agreement
P - 17. UNANIMOUSLY	Q. Excuse
J - 18. PREEMINENT	R. Scornfully
F - 19. FILIAL	S. Gave up all resistance
S - 20. CAPITULATED	T. Critical; of supreme importance
V - 21. TYRANNY	U. Not rehearsed; on the spur of the moment
I - 22. POSTHUMOUSLY	V. Absolute power; esp. when used unjustly or cruelly
N - 23. RETINUE	W. Disputes
Y - 24. IGNOMINIOUS	X. Happening at the same time
C - 25. EMBOLDENED	Y. Disgraceful; shameful

Animal Farm Vocabulary Matching 2

___ 1. VIVACIOUS A. Drunkards
___ 2. FALTER B. Disputes
___ 3. UNANIMOUSLY C. Befitting a son or daughter
___ 4. CONTROVERSIES D. Sum of money paid as a retirement benefit
___ 5. RETINUE E. Disgraceful; shameful
___ 6. PRETEXT F. Encouraged; made brave; gave courage to
___ 7. OBSTINATE G. Lack of interest or emotion
___ 8. CAPITULATED H. Waver in confidence; hesitate; fail
___ 9. CYNICAL I. Stubbornly inflexible
___10. PERPETUALLY J. Outstanding
___11. PREEMINENT K. Continually
___12. PENSION L. Bitterly mocking
___13. CONCILIATORY M. Untiring; tireless
___14. IMPROMPTU N. Absolute power; esp. when used unjustly or cruelly
___15. EMBOLDENED O. Lively; spirited
___16. TYRANNY P. Astute; clever
___17. IGNOMINIOUS Q. Scornfully
___18. FILIAL R. Those accompanying a person of rank
___19. TUMULT S. Showing good-will; peace-making
___20. LURKING T. In complete agreement
___21. INDEFATIGABLE U. Exist concealed or unsuspected
___22. INEBRIATES V. Excuse
___23. CONTEMPTUOUSLY W. Gave up all resistance
___24. APATHY X. Commotion
___25. SHREWD Y. Not rehearsed; on the spur of the moment

Animal Farm Vocabulary Matching 2 Answer Key

O - 1. VIVACIOUS		A. Drunkards
H - 2. FALTER		B. Disputes
T - 3. UNANIMOUSLY		C. Befitting a son or daughter
B - 4. CONTROVERSIES		D. Sum of money paid as a retirement benefit
R - 5. RETINUE		E. Disgraceful; shameful
V - 6. PRETEXT		F. Encouraged; made brave; gave courage to
I - 7. OBSTINATE		G. Lack of interest or emotion
W - 8. CAPITULATED		H. Waver in confidence; hesitate; fail
L - 9. CYNICAL		I. Stubbornly inflexible
K - 10. PERPETUALLY		J. Outstanding
J - 11. PREEMINENT		K. Continually
D - 12. PENSION		L. Bitterly mocking
S - 13. CONCILIATORY		M. Untiring; tireless
Y - 14. IMPROMPTU		N. Absolute power; esp. when used unjustly or cruelly
F - 15. EMBOLDENED		O. Lively; spirited
N - 16. TYRANNY		P. Astute; clever
E - 17. IGNOMINIOUS		Q. Scornfully
C - 18. FILIAL		R. Those accompanying a person of rank
X - 19. TUMULT		S. Showing good-will; peace-making
U - 20. LURKING		T. In complete agreement
M - 21. INDEFATIGABLE		U. Exist concealed or unsuspected
A - 22. INEBRIATES		V. Excuse
Q - 23. CONTEMPTUOUSLY		W. Gave up all resistance
G - 24. APATHY		X. Commotion
P - 25. SHREWD		Y. Not rehearsed; on the spur of the moment

Animal Farm Vocabulary Matching 3

___ 1. IGNOMINIOUS   A. After one's death
___ 2. CRUCIAL   B. In complete agreement
___ 3. IMPROMPTU   C. Waver in confidence; hesitate; fail
___ 4. SOLEMNLY   D. About to take place
___ 5. APATHY   E. Disgraceful; shameful
___ 6. INEBRIATES   F. Happening at the same time
___ 7. UNANIMOUSLY   G. Encouraged; made brave; gave courage to
___ 8. SUPERANNUATED   H. Lively; spirited
___ 9. SIMULTANEOUSLY   I. Impossible to control or restrain
___10. PREEMINENT   J. Critical; of supreme importance
___11. SHREWD   K. Astute; clever
___12. CYNICAL   L. Those accompanying a person of rank
___13. IRREPRESSIBLE   M. Lack of interest or emotion
___14. EMBOLDENED   N. Seriously; deeply earnest
___15. PENSION   O. Showing good-will; peace-making
___16. PRETEXT   P. Sum of money paid as a retirement benefit
___17. IMPENDING   Q. Stubbornly inflexible
___18. OBSTINATE   R. Not rehearsed; on the spur of the moment
___19. INDEFATIGABLE   S. Disputes
___20. FALTER   T. Outstanding
___21. CONTROVERSIES   U. Untiring; tireless
___22. VIVACIOUS   V. Retired because of age or infirmity
___23. POSTHUMOUSLY   W. Drunkards
___24. CONCILIATORY   X. Bitterly mocking
___25. RETINUE   Y. Excuse

Animal Farm Vocabulary Matching 3 Answer Key

- E - 1. IGNOMINIOUS
- J - 2. CRUCIAL
- R - 3. IMPROMPTU
- N - 4. SOLEMNLY
- M - 5. APATHY
- W - 6. INEBRIATES
- B - 7. UNANIMOUSLY
- V - 8. SUPERANNUATED
- F - 9. SIMULTANEOUSLY
- T - 10. PREEMINENT
- K - 11. SHREWD
- X - 12. CYNICAL
- I - 13. IRREPRESSIBLE
- G - 14. EMBOLDENED
- P - 15. PENSION
- Y - 16. PRETEXT
- D - 17. IMPENDING
- Q - 18. OBSTINATE
- U - 19. INDEFATIGABLE
- C - 20. FALTER
- S - 21. CONTROVERSIES
- H - 22. VIVACIOUS
- A - 23. POSTHUMOUSLY
- O - 24. CONCILIATORY
- L - 25. RETINUE

A. After one's death
B. In complete agreement
C. Waver in confidence; hesitate; fail
D. About to take place
E. Disgraceful; shameful
F. Happening at the same time
G. Encouraged; made brave; gave courage to
H. Lively; spirited
I. Impossible to control or restrain
J. Critical; of supreme importance
K. Astute; clever
L. Those accompanying a person of rank
M. Lack of interest or emotion
N. Seriously; deeply earnest
O. Showing good-will; peace-making
P. Sum of money paid as a retirement benefit
Q. Stubbornly inflexible
R. Not rehearsed; on the spur of the moment
S. Disputes
T. Outstanding
U. Untiring; tireless
V. Retired because of age or infirmity
W. Drunkards
X. Bitterly mocking
Y. Excuse

Animal Farm Vocabulary Matching 4

___ 1. CYNICAL   A. Waver in confidence; hesitate; fail
___ 2. UNANIMOUSLY   B. Disputes
___ 3. CONCILIATORY   C. Outstanding
___ 4. POSTHUMOUSLY   D. Not rehearsed; on the spur of the moment
___ 5. FALTER   E. Bitterly mocking
___ 6. PRETEXT   F. Critical; of supreme importance
___ 7. CRUCIAL   G. Happening at the same time
___ 8. IMPENDING   H. Exist concealed or unsuspected
___ 9. IRREPRESSIBLE   I. Impossible to control or restrain
___10. INDEFATIGABLE   J. Facial expression
___11. PENSION   K. Befitting a son or daughter
___12. INEBRIATES   L. Absolute power; esp. when used unjustly or cruelly
___13. RETINUE   M. About to take place
___14. TYRANNY   N. Drunkards
___15. COUNTENANCE   O. Sum of money paid as a retirement benefit
___16. EMBOLDENED   P. After one's death
___17. FILIAL   Q. Untiring; tireless
___18. CONTROVERSIES   R. Scornfully
___19. IMPROMPTU   S. Disgraceful; shameful
___20. PREEMINENT   T. Excuse
___21. IGNOMINIOUS   U. Those accompanying a person of rank
___22. SIMULTANEOUSLY   V. Continually
___23. CONTEMPTUOUSLY   W. Showing good-will; peace-making
___24. LURKING   X. Encouraged; made brave; gave courage to
___25. PERPETUALLY   Y. In complete agreement

Animal Farm Vocabulary Matching 4 Answer Key

E - 1. CYNICAL		A. Waver in confidence; hesitate; fail
Y - 2. UNANIMOUSLY		B. Disputes
W - 3. CONCILIATORY		C. Outstanding
P - 4. POSTHUMOUSLY		D. Not rehearsed; on the spur of the moment
A - 5. FALTER		E. Bitterly mocking
T - 6. PRETEXT		F. Critical; of supreme importance
F - 7. CRUCIAL		G. Happening at the same time
M - 8. IMPENDING		H. Exist concealed or unsuspected
I - 9. IRREPRESSIBLE		I. Impossible to control or restrain
Q - 10. INDEFATIGABLE		J. Facial expression
O - 11. PENSION		K. Befitting a son or daughter
N - 12. INEBRIATES		L. Absolute power; esp. when used unjustly or cruelly
U - 13. RETINUE		M. About to take place
L - 14. TYRANNY		N. Drunkards
J - 15. COUNTENANCE		O. Sum of money paid as a retirement benefit
X - 16. EMBOLDENED		P. After one's death
K - 17. FILIAL		Q. Untiring; tireless
B - 18. CONTROVERSIES		R. Scornfully
D - 19. IMPROMPTU		S. Disgraceful; shameful
C - 20. PREEMINENT		T. Excuse
S - 21. IGNOMINIOUS		U. Those accompanying a person of rank
G - 22. SIMULTANEOUSLY		V. Continually
R - 23. CONTEMPTUOUSLY		W. Showing good-will; peace-making
H - 24. LURKING		X. Encouraged; made brave; gave courage to
V - 25. PERPETUALLY		Y. In complete agreement

Animal Farm Vocabulary Magic Squares 1

Match the definition with the vocabulary word. Put your answers in the magic squares below. When your answers are correct, all columns and rows will add to the same number.

A. CONCILIATORY
B. UNANIMOUSLY
C. RETINUE
D. APATHY
E. CAPITULATED
F. INDEFATIGABLE
G. LURKING
H. EMBOLDENED
I. IMPENDING
J. SUPERANNUATED
K. PREEMINENT
L. PRETEXT
M. COUNTENANCE
N. TYRANNY
O. PENSION
P. IGNOMINIOUS

1. In complete agreement
2. Exist concealed or unsuspected
3. Outstanding
4. Absolute power; esp. when used unjustly or cruelly
5. Facial expression
6. Excuse
7. Encouraged; made brave; gave courage to
8. Showing good-will; peace-making
9. Disgraceful; shameful
10. About to take place
11. Gave up all resistance
12. Lack of interest or emotion
13. Those accompanying a person of rank
14. Untiring; tireless
15. Retired because of age or infirmity
16. Sum of money paid as a retirement benefit

A=	B=	C=	D=
E=	F=	G=	H=
I=	J=	K=	L=
M=	N=	O=	P=

Animal Farm Vocabulary Magic Squares 1 Answer Key

Match the definition with the vocabulary word. Put your answers in the magic squares below. When your answers are correct, all columns and rows will add to the same number.

A. CONCILIATORY
B. UNANIMOUSLY
C. RETINUE
D. APATHY
E. CAPITULATED
F. INDEFATIGABLE
G. LURKING
H. EMBOLDENED
I. IMPENDING
J. SUPERANNUATED
K. PREEMINENT
L. PRETEXT
M. COUNTENANCE
N. TYRANNY
O. PENSION
P. IGNOMINIOUS

1. In complete agreement
2. Exist concealed or unsuspected
3. Outstanding
4. Absolute power; esp. when used unjustly or cruelly
5. Facial expression
6. Excuse
7. Encouraged; made brave; gave courage to
8. Showing good-will; peace-making
9. Disgraceful; shameful
10. About to take place
11. Gave up all resistance
12. Lack of interest or emotion
13. Those accompanying a person of rank
14. Untiring; tireless
15. Retired because of age or infirmity
16. Sum of money paid as a retirement benefit

A=8	B=1	C=13	D=12
E=11	F=14	G=2	H=7
I=10	J=15	K=3	L=6
M=5	N=4	O=16	P=9

Animal Farm Vocabulary Magic Squares 2

Match the definition with the vocabulary word. Put your answers in the magic squares below. When your answers are correct, all columns and rows will add to the same number.

A. RETINUE
B. EMBOLDENED
C. TUMULT
D. SUPERANNUATED
E. POSTHUMOUSLY
F. CYNICAL
G. LURKING
H. CONTEMPTUOUSLY
I. TYRANNY
J. PENSION
K. PRETEXT
L. INDEFATIGABLE
M. INEBRIATES
N. SHREWD
O. IMPROMPTU
P. UNANIMOUSLY

1. Commotion
2. Sum of money paid as a retirement benefit
3. Bitterly mocking
4. Not rehearsed; on the spur of the moment
5. In complete agreement
6. After one's death
7. Absolute power; esp. when used unjustly or cruelly
8. Retired because of age or infirmity
9. Drunkards
10. Scornfully
11. Untiring; tireless
12. Those accompanying a person of rank
13. Encouraged; made brave; gave courage to
14. Excuse
15. Exist concealed or unsuspected
16. Astute; clever

A=	B=	C=	D=
E=	F=	G=	H=
I=	J=	K=	L=
M=	N=	O=	P=

Animal Farm Vocabulary Magic Squares 2 Answer Key

Match the definition with the vocabulary word. Put your answers in the magic squares below. When your answers are correct, all columns and rows will add to the same number.

A. RETINUE
B. EMBOLDENED
C. TUMULT
D. SUPERANNUATED
E. POSTHUMOUSLY
F. CYNICAL
G. LURKING
H. CONTEMPTUOUSLY
I. TYRANNY
J. PENSION
K. PRETEXT
L. INDEFATIGABLE
M. INEBRIATES
N. SHREWD
O. IMPROMPTU
P. UNANIMOUSLY

1. Commotion
2. Sum of money paid as a retirement benefit
3. Bitterly mocking
4. Not rehearsed; on the spur of the moment
5. In complete agreement
6. After one's death
7. Absolute power; esp. when used unjustly or cruelly
8. Retired because of age or infirmity
9. Drunkards
10. Scornfully
11. Untiring; tireless
12. Those accompanying a person of rank
13. Encouraged; made brave; gave courage to
14. Excuse
15. Exist concealed or unsuspected
16. Astute; clever

A=12	B=13	C=1	D=8
E=6	F=3	G=15	H=10
I=7	J=2	K=14	L=11
M=9	N=16	O=4	P=5

Animal Farm Vocabulary Magic Squares 3

Match the definition with the vocabulary word. Put your answers in the magic squares below. When your answers are correct, all columns and rows will add to the same number.

A. RETINUE
B. SOLEMNLY
C. LURKING
D. SIMULTANEOUSLY
E. POSTHUMOUSLY
F. IMPROMPTU
G. COUNTENANCE
H. FILIAL
I. UNANIMOUSLY
J. VIVACIOUS
K. EMBOLDENED
L. FALTER
M. CONTROVERSIES
N. SUPERANNUATED
O. PERPETUALLY
P. CRUCIAL

1. Befitting a son or daughter
2. Disputes
3. Seriously; deeply earnest
4. Encouraged; made brave; gave courage to
5. Lively; spirited
6. Exist concealed or unsuspected
7. Critical; of supreme importance
8. After one's death
9. Continually
10. Not rehearsed; on the spur of the moment
11. In complete agreement
12. Happening at the same time
13. Those accompanying a person of rank
14. Waver in confidence; hesitate; fail
15. Facial expression
16. Retired because of age or infirmity

A=	B=	C=	D=
E=	F=	G=	H=
I=	J=	K=	L=
M=	N=	O=	P=

Animal Farm Vocabulary Magic Squares 3 Answer Key

Match the definition with the vocabulary word. Put your answers in the magic squares below. When your answers are correct, all columns and rows will add to the same number.

A. RETINUE
B. SOLEMNLY
C. LURKING
D. SIMULTANEOUSLY
E. POSTHUMOUSLY
F. IMPROMPTU
G. COUNTENANCE
H. FILIAL
I. UNANIMOUSLY
J. VIVACIOUS
K. EMBOLDENED
L. FALTER
M. CONTROVERSIES
N. SUPERANNUATED
O. PERPETUALLY
P. CRUCIAL

1. Befitting a son or daughter
2. Disputes
3. Seriously; deeply earnest
4. Encouraged; made brave; gave courage to
5. Lively; spirited
6. Exist concealed or unsuspected
7. Critical; of supreme importance
8. After one's death
9. Continually
10. Not rehearsed; on the spur of the moment
11. In complete agreement
12. Happening at the same time
13. Those accompanying a person of rank
14. Waver in confidence; hesitate; fail
15. Facial expression
16. Retired because of age or infirmity

A=13	B=3	C=6	D=12
E=8	F=10	G=15	H=1
I=11	J=5	K=4	L=14
M=2	N=16	O=9	P=7

Animal Farm Vocabulary Magic Squares 4

Match the definition with the vocabulary word. Put your answers in the magic squares below. When your answers are correct, all columns and rows will add to the same number.

A. PRETEXT
B. VIVACIOUS
C. PERPETUALLY
D. PREEMINENT
E. COUNTENANCE
F. CRUCIAL
G. SIMULTANEOUSLY
H. TYRANNY
I. IMPENDING
J. APATHY
K. FILIAL
L. INEBRIATES
M. SOLEMNLY
N. CYNICAL
O. SHREWD
P. RETINUE

1. Critical; of supreme importance
2. About to take place
3. Astute; clever
4. Outstanding
5. Seriously; deeply earnest
6. Lively; spirited
7. Absolute power; esp. when used unjustly or cruelly
8. Befitting a son or daughter
9. Continually
10. Those accompanying a person of rank
11. Lack of interest or emotion
12. Facial expression
13. Drunkards
14. Happening at the same time
15. Excuse
16. Bitterly mocking

A=	B=	C=	D=
E=	F=	G=	H=
I=	J=	K=	L=
M=	N=	O=	P=

Animal Farm Vocabulary Magic Squares 4 Answer Key

Match the definition with the vocabulary word. Put your answers in the magic squares below. When your answers are correct, all columns and rows will add to the same number.

A. PRETEXT
B. VIVACIOUS
C. PERPETUALLY
D. PREEMINENT
E. COUNTENANCE
F. CRUCIAL
G. SIMULTANEOUSLY
H. TYRANNY
I. IMPENDING
J. APATHY
K. FILIAL
L. INEBRIATES
M. SOLEMNLY
N. CYNICAL
O. SHREWD
P. RETINUE

1. Critical; of supreme importance
2. About to take place
3. Astute; clever
4. Outstanding
5. Seriously; deeply earnest
6. Lively; spirited
7. Absolute power; esp. when used unjustly or cruelly
8. Befitting a son or daughter
9. Continually
10. Those accompanying a person of rank
11. Lack of interest or emotion
12. Facial expression
13. Drunkards
14. Happening at the same time
15. Excuse
16. Bitterly mocking

A=15	B=6	C=9	D=4
E=12	F=1	G=14	H=7
I=2	J=11	K=8	L=13
M=5	N=16	O=3	P=10

Animal Farm Vocabulary Word Search 1

```
C Y N I C A L S U P E R A N N U A T E D
Q S C X M Y T U G C Y M C S N C P Z E R
K P O W S X H N R Y A B V A P Y C C L B
M K N B E I I J Q K F P N M R N N A R L
L H T T S D M K L K I I O V A I U E W
X X E G N T K U D N M N T T N C T W L Z
J R M E Z J I Z L O M A G E U P S S B N
P D P H N M K N U T I Z T R M L U S I Y
M M T L M H Q S A L A N C O T O A G S Q
I T U L L F L R I T U N R N I C N T S H
F Y O S R Y J C E O E P E C W O K P E D
I R U O Y J N N C T M N A O M K G S R D
L A S L F O O S M I I V T I U N C Y P R
I N L E C I L H J M I N N U S S H J E J
A N Y M S X Z R E V H I U L M T L T R T
L Y J N D E N E D L O B M E A U L Y R N
H S E L L V R W V U F W F P R A L T I Z
M P N Y Z P S D S J R G A F F Q L T H Z
```

About to take place (9)
Absolute power; esp. when used unjustly or cruelly (7)
Astute; clever (6)
Befitting a son or daughter (6)
Bitterly mocking (7)
Commotion (6)
Critical; of supreme importance (7)
Disgraceful; shameful (11)
Encouraged; made brave; gave courage to (10)
Excuse (7)
Exist concealed or unsuspected (7)
Facial expression (11)
Gave up all resistance (11)
Happening at the same time (14)
Impossible to control or restrain (13)
In complete agreement (11)
Lack of interest or emotion (6)
Lively; spirited (9)
Not rehearsed; on the spur of the moment (9)
Outstanding (10)
Retired because of age or infirmity (13)
Scornfully (14)
Seriously; deeply earnest (8)
Showing good-will; peace-making (12)
Stubbornly inflexible (9)
Sum of money paid as a retirement benefit (7)
Those accompanying a person of rank (7)
Waver in confidence; hesitate; fail (6)

Animal Farm Vocabulary Word Search 1 Answer Key

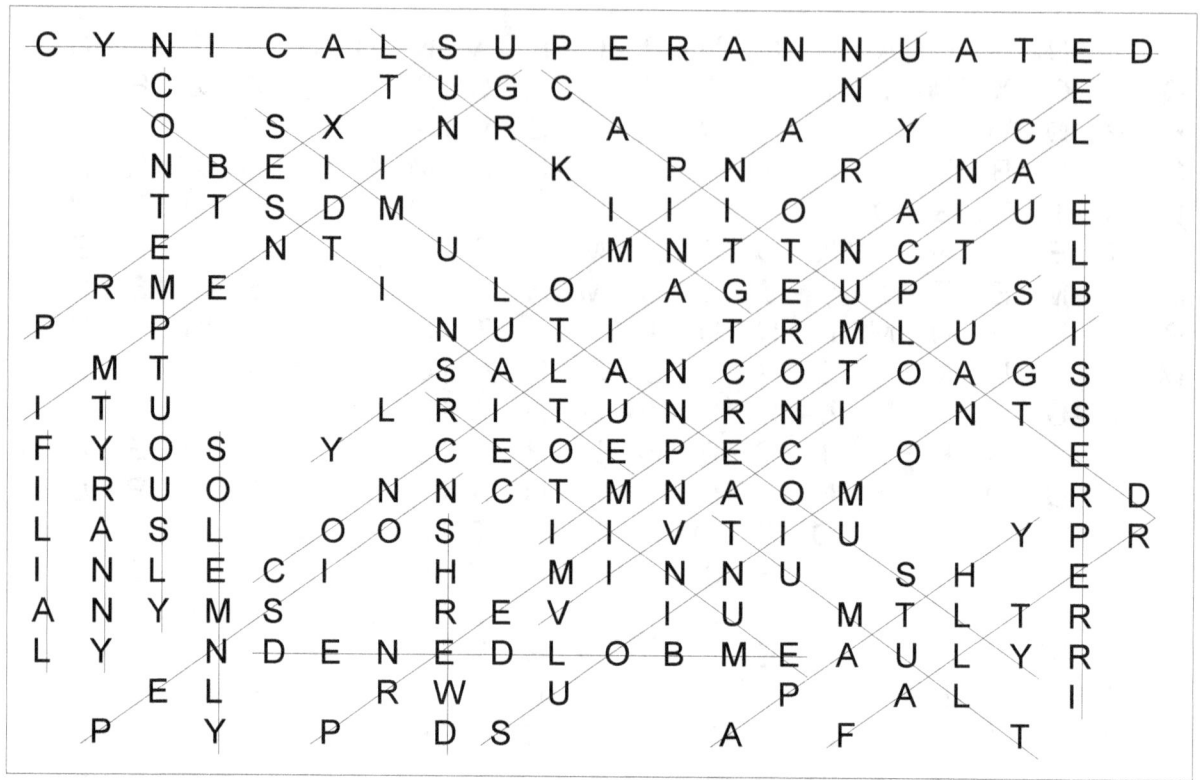

About to take place (9)
Absolute power; esp. when used unjustly or cruelly (7)
Astute; clever (6)
Befitting a son or daughter (6)
Bitterly mocking (7)
Commotion (6)
Critical; of supreme importance (7)
Disgraceful; shameful (11)
Encouraged; made brave; gave courage to (10)
Excuse (7)
Exist concealed or unsuspected (7)
Facial expression (11)
Gave up all resistance (11)
Happening at the same time (14)
Impossible to control or restrain (13)
In complete agreement (11)
Lack of interest or emotion (6)

Lively; spirited (9)
Not rehearsed; on the spur of the moment (9)
Outstanding (10)
Retired because of age or infirmity (13)
Scornfully (14)
Seriously; deeply earnest (8)
Showing good-will; peace-making (12)
Stubbornly inflexible (9)
Sum of money paid as a retirement benefit (7)
Those accompanying a person of rank (7)
Waver in confidence; hesitate; fail (6)

Animal Farm Vocabulary Word Search 2

```
C Y L L A U T E P R E P E K A L H W H S
O Z P G P P N D U W B M L S M P J F D N
U B J R Q N G V J N L N B W H C A F J N
N M O R E T J B J Z A G A O A P T T X G
T Y B B K T Y S J M Q N G P L L D N H L
E L B I S S E R P E R R I P G D R W T Y
N S C M M T F X A N B T T M E N E U T L
A U Q Y G P I G T N U X A F O N M N V K
N O K H N D R N G L N R F G I U S G E D
C U K K I I P O A W Q Y E C L L S I W D
E T D V K Z C T M T F Y D T R V I L O Y
L P T Y R Y E A Q P E F N S I U C A Y N
F M S M U D P F L T T R I W H N C J L H
G E W H L B Y S Y D E U R N Q R U I P T
M T R M R D S S E T A I R B E N I E A S
R N S O L E M N L Y I M P E N D I N G L
J O N B W R W A P R E E M I N E N T M D
S C R R S N F D V I V A C I O U S C J T
```

About to take place (9)
Absolute power; esp. when used unjustly or cruelly (7)
Astute; clever (6)
Befitting a son or daughter (6)
Bitterly mocking (7)
Commotion (6)
Continually (11)
Critical; of supreme importance (7)
Drunkards (10)
Encouraged; made brave; gave courage to (10)
Excuse (7)
Exist concealed or unsuspected (7)
Facial expression (11)
Gave up all resistance (11)
Impossible to control or restrain (13)
In complete agreement (11)
Lack of interest or emotion (6)

Lively; spirited (9)
Not rehearsed; on the spur of the moment (9)
Outstanding (10)
Scornfully (14)
Seriously; deeply earnest (8)
Stubbornly inflexible (9)
Sum of money paid as a retirement benefit (7)
Those accompanying a person of rank (7)
Untiring; tireless (13)
Waver in confidence; hesitate; fail (6)

Animal Farm Vocabulary Word Search 2 Answer Key

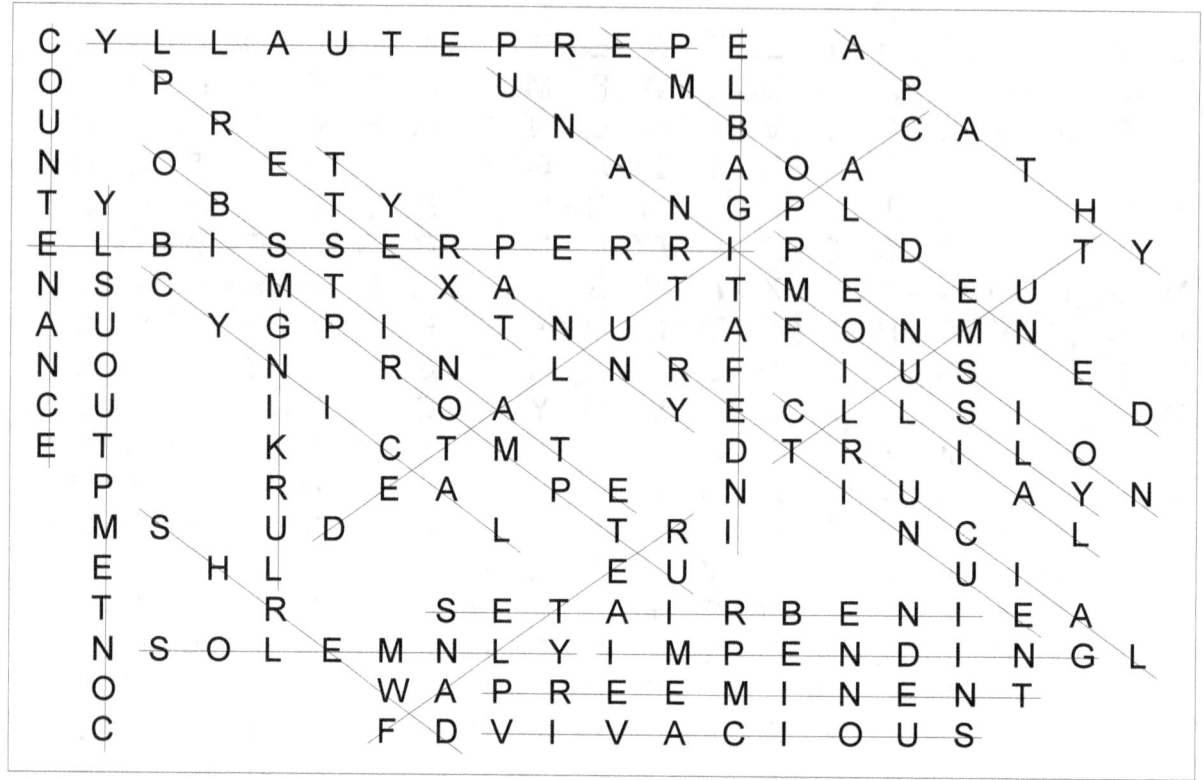

About to take place (9)
Absolute power; esp. when used unjustly or cruelly (7)
Astute; clever (6)
Befitting a son or daughter (6)
Bitterly mocking (7)
Commotion (6)
Continually (11)
Critical; of supreme importance (7)
Drunkards (10)
Encouraged; made brave; gave courage to (10)
Excuse (7)
Exist concealed or unsuspected (7)
Facial expression (11)
Gave up all resistance (11)
Impossible to control or restrain (13)
In complete agreement (11)
Lack of interest or emotion (6)

Lively; spirited (9)
Not rehearsed; on the spur of the moment (9)
Outstanding (10)
Scornfully (14)
Seriously; deeply earnest (8)
Stubbornly inflexible (9)
Sum of money paid as a retirement benefit (7)
Those accompanying a person of rank (7)
Untiring; tireless (13)
Waver in confidence; hesitate; fail (6)

Animal Farm Vocabulary Word Search 3

```
E M B O L D E N E D Y C R U C I A L S S
U O I S B T N B D L Y Z J E J K W U H D
N B N E Q K S R N W D T C Y T E O G R N
A S D L S Z Z M A P A T H Y C I G V E D
N T E B Q I E R S X S H P N C Y N L W B
I I F I Y L M X G C X Y A A H D I U D P
M N A S O X I U T K T N V H T J D P E V
O A T S Q I S N L D E I Z X D V N E W S
U T I E D K M Z E T V X S B N P E R D W
S E G R S V Z P N B A F K F R X P P L L
L N A P H W V U R W R N J E Z K M E W T
Y N B E G P O L G O C I E D N V I T T K
N Y L R N C R F P Y M M A O B W T U F Q
N L E R I W S E N H I P I T U S V A I K
A L B I K P D I T N P S T Q E S S L L C
R T X K R V C Z E E N X C U B S L L I H
Y H P Q U A D N Y E X F A L T E R Y A Q
T U M U L T T P P O S T H U M O U S L Y
```

About to take place (9)
Absolute power; esp. when used unjustly or cruelly (7)
After one's death (12)
Astute; clever (6)
Befitting a son or daughter (6)
Bitterly mocking (7)
Commotion (6)
Continually (11)
Critical; of supreme importance (7)
Drunkards (10)
Encouraged; made brave; gave courage to (10)
Excuse (7)
Exist concealed or unsuspected (7)
Facial expression (11)
Happening at the same time (14)
Impossible to control or restrain (13)
In complete agreement (11)

Lack of interest or emotion (6)
Lively; spirited (9)
Not rehearsed; on the spur of the moment (9)
Outstanding (10)
Seriously; deeply earnest (8)
Stubbornly inflexible (9)
Sum of money paid as a retirement benefit (7)
Those accompanying a person of rank (7)
Untiring; tireless (13)
Waver in confidence; hesitate; fail (6)

Animal Farm Vocabulary Word Search 3 Answer Key

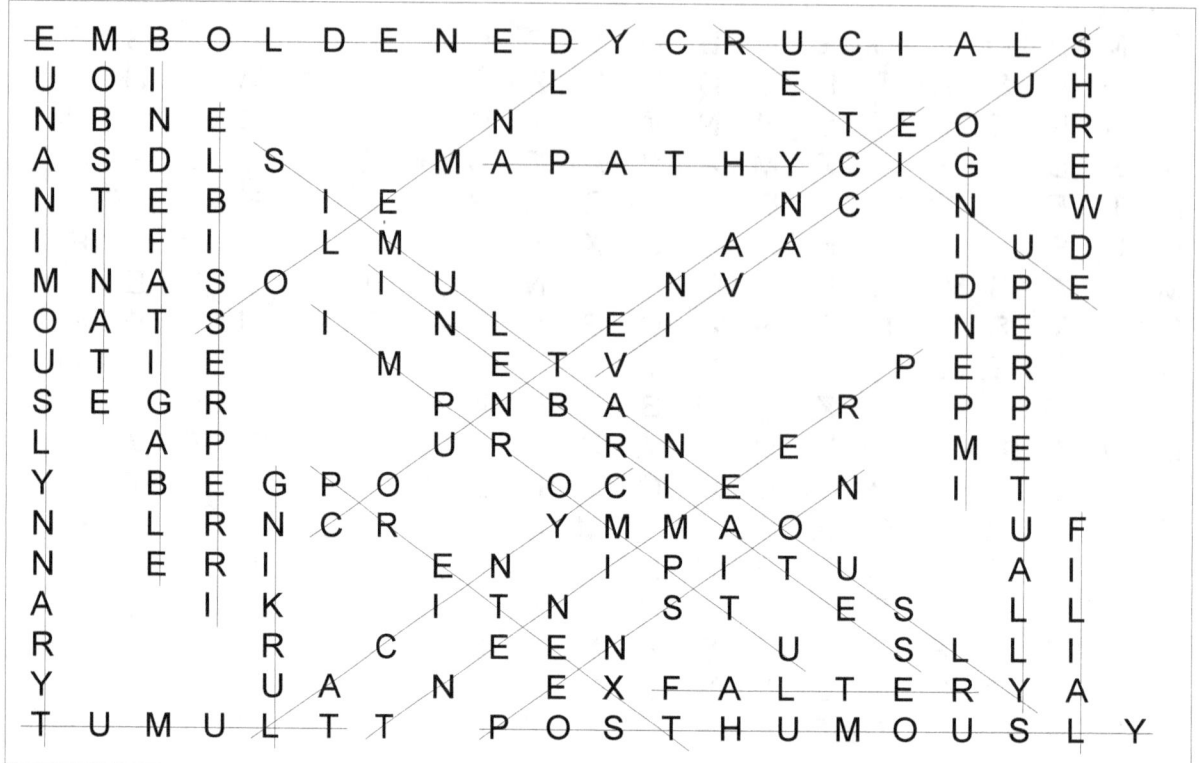

About to take place (9)
Absolute power; esp. when used unjustly or cruelly (7)
After one's death (12)
Astute; clever (6)
Befitting a son or daughter (6)
Bitterly mocking (7)
Commotion (6)
Continually (11)
Critical; of supreme importance (7)
Drunkards (10)
Encouraged; made brave; gave courage to (10)
Excuse (7)
Exist concealed or unsuspected (7)
Facial expression (11)
Happening at the same time (14)
Impossible to control or restrain (13)
In complete agreement (11)

Lack of interest or emotion (6)
Lively; spirited (9)
Not rehearsed; on the spur of the moment (9)
Outstanding (10)
Seriously; deeply earnest (8)
Stubbornly inflexible (9)
Sum of money paid as a retirement benefit (7)
Those accompanying a person of rank (7)
Untiring; tireless (13)
Waver in confidence; hesitate; fail (6)

Animal Farm Vocabulary Word Search 4

```
O B S T I N A T E P Y P R S F P L T N G
C I R N P C P K C G L Z J H I O U U F P
S M S E H R J E S Y S Z S R L S R M I Y
P P U N Z U E P R P N E F E I T K U N T
M R P I R C P T T P T I H W A H I L D D
S O E M D I C W E A E C D L U N T E R
H M R E Z A Y O I X M T S A N M G V F B
C P A E F L F R N B T M U C L O V I A X
O T N R N G B K O C P Z L A Z U W V T D
U U N P H E V L F G I W X R L S C A I H
N V U R N R D P S S O L E M N L Y C G T
T L A I H E G E Y R E A I Z D Y Y I A M
E H T D N T P N P U B X P A S K V O B Y
N X E E G L K S N D T Q W A T M M U L C
A F D U N A N I M O U S L Y T O V S E V
N H J R D F T O J V X N F N L H R V V L
C V Q F M E G N I D N E P M I V Y Y C C
E Q T Y R A N N Y C A P I T U L A T E D
```

About to take place (9)
Absolute power; esp. when used unjustly or cruelly (7)
After one's death (12)
Astute; clever (6)
Befitting a son or daughter (6)
Bitterly mocking (7)
Commotion (6)
Continually (11)
Critical; of supreme importance (7)
Drunkards (10)
Encouraged; made brave; gave courage to (10)
Excuse (7)
Exist concealed or unsuspected (7)
Facial expression (11)
Gave up all resistance (11)
In complete agreement (11)
Lack of interest or emotion (6)

Lively; spirited (9)
Not rehearsed; on the spur of the moment (9)
Outstanding (10)
Retired because of age or infirmity (13)
Seriously; deeply earnest (8)
Showing good-will; peace-making (12)
Stubbornly inflexible (9)
Sum of money paid as a retirement benefit (7)
Those accompanying a person of rank (7)
Untiring; tireless (13)
Waver in confidence; hesitate; fail (6)

Animal Farm Vocabulary Word Search 4 Answer Key

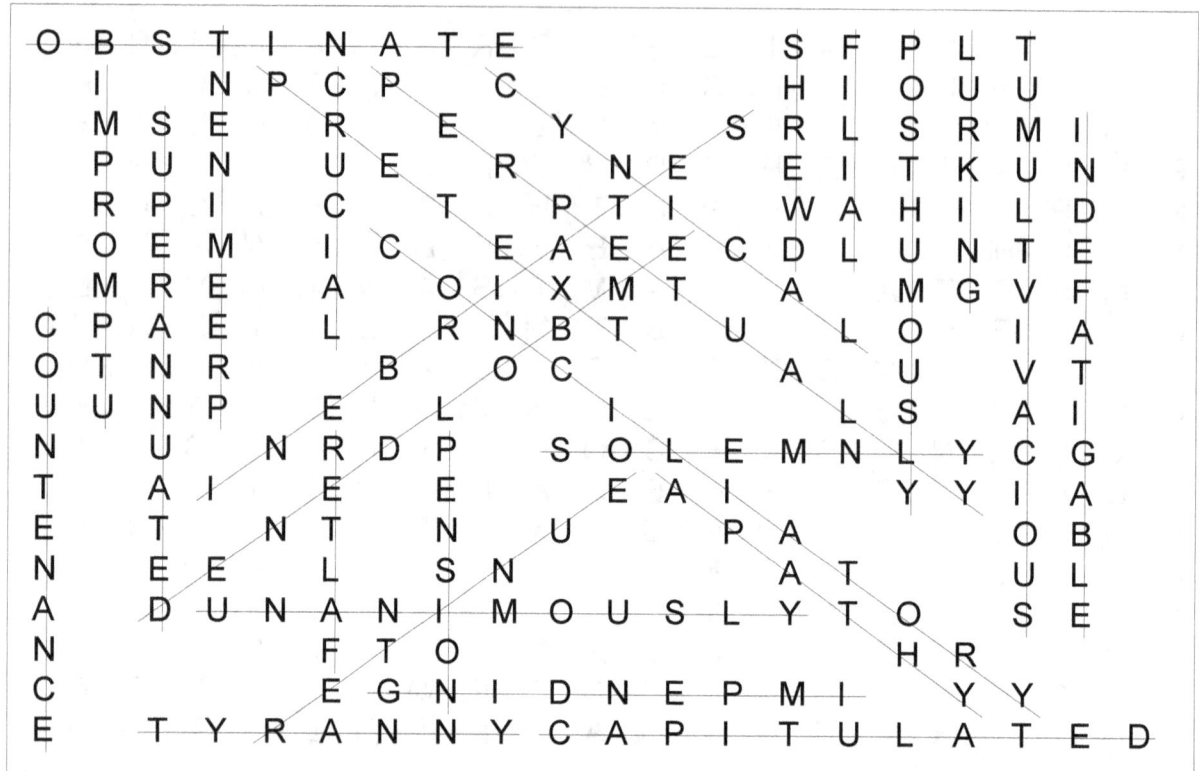

About to take place (9)
Absolute power; esp. when used unjustly or cruelly (7)
After one's death (12)
Astute; clever (6)
Befitting a son or daughter (6)
Bitterly mocking (7)
Commotion (6)
Continually (11)
Critical; of supreme importance (7)
Drunkards (10)
Encouraged; made brave; gave courage to (10)
Excuse (7)
Exist concealed or unsuspected (7)
Facial expression (11)
Gave up all resistance (11)
In complete agreement (11)
Lack of interest or emotion (6)

Lively; spirited (9)
Not rehearsed; on the spur of the moment (9)
Outstanding (10)
Retired because of age or infirmity (13)
Seriously; deeply earnest (8)
Showing good-will; peace-making (12)
Stubbornly inflexible (9)
Sum of money paid as a retirement benefit (7)
Those accompanying a person of rank (7)
Untiring; tireless (13)
Waver in confidence; hesitate; fail (6)

Animal Farm Vocabuary Crossword 1

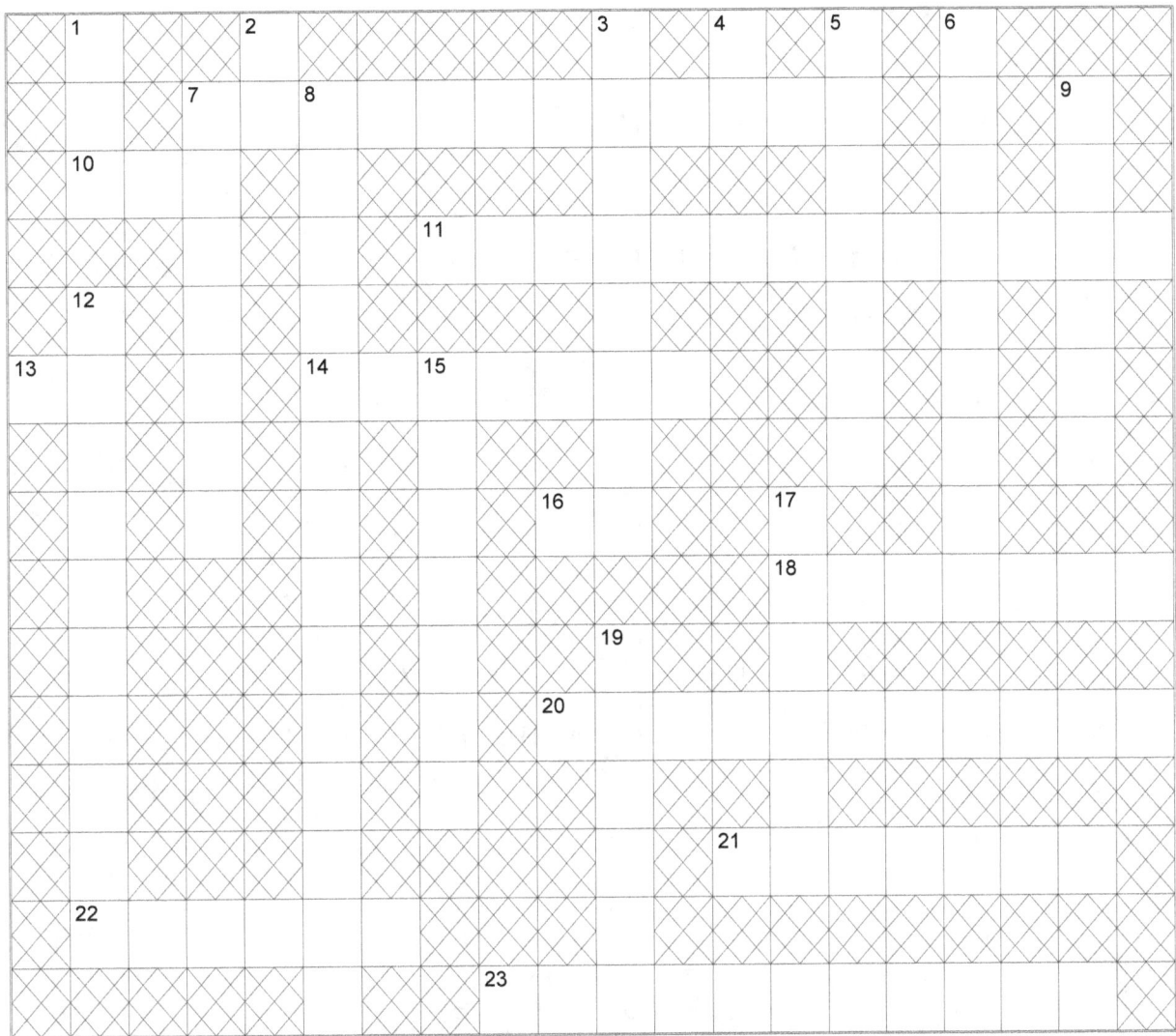

Across
7. After one's death
10. Belonging to us
11. Untiring; tireless
13. Either's partner
14. Exist concealed or unsuspected
16. Belonging to me
18. Sum of money paid as a retirement benefit
20. Gave up all resistance
21. Absolute power; esp. when used unjustly or cruelly
22. Commotion
23. Continually

Down
1. Also
2. A negative answer
3. Seriously; deeply earnest
4. Ourselves
5. Bitterly mocking
6. Lively; spirited
7. Excuse
8. Happening at the same time
9. Befitting a son or daughter
12. Outstanding
15. Those accompanying a person of rank
17. Lack of interest or emotion
19. Waver in confidence; hesitate; fail

Animal Farm Vcoabulary Crossword 1 Anwer Key

Across
- 7. After one's death
- 10. Belonging to us
- 11. Untiring; tireless
- 13. Either's partner
- 14. Exist concealed or unsuspected
- 16. Belonging to me
- 18. Sum of money paid as a retirement benefit
- 20. Gave up all resistance
- 21. Absolute power; esp. when used unjustly or cruelly
- 22. Commotion
- 23. Continually

Down
- 1. Also
- 2. A negative answer
- 3. Seriously; deeply earnest
- 4. Ourselves
- 5. Bitterly mocking
- 6. Lively; spirited
- 7. Excuse
- 8. Happening at the same time
- 9. Befitting a son or daughter
- 12. Outstanding
- 15. Those accompanying a person of rank
- 17. Lack of interest or emotion
- 19. Waver in confidence; hesitate; fail

Animal Farm Vocabulary Crossword 2

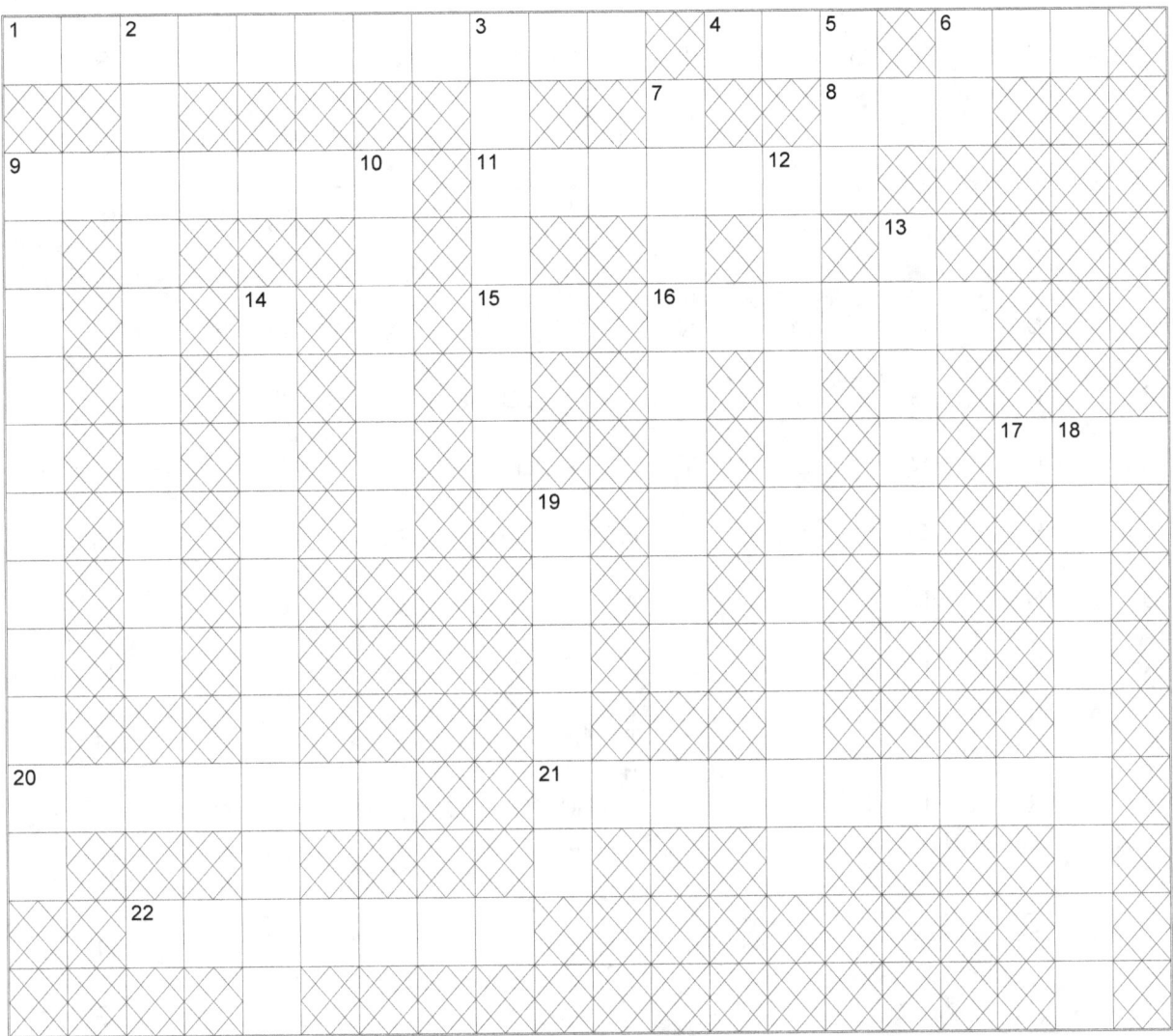

Across
1. Gave up all resistance
4. Also
6. Belonging to us
8. Neither's partner
9. Excuse
11. Those accompanying a person of rank
15. A negative answer
16. Lack of interest or emotion
17. Belonging to him
20. Exist concealed or unsuspected
21. Encouraged; made brave; gave courage to
22. Critical; of supreme importance

Down
2. Outstanding
3. Absolute power; esp. when used unjustly or cruelly
5. First number
6. Either's partner
7. Lively; spirited
9. Continually
10. Commotion
12. In complete agreement
13. Astute; clever
14. Disgraceful; shameful
18. About to take place
19. Waver in confidence; hesitate; fail

Animal Farm Vocabulary Crossword 2 Answer Key

	1 C	2 A	P	I	T	U	L	3 A	T	E	D		4 T	5 O	O		6 O	U	R	
		R						Y			7 V		8 N	O	R					
9 P	R	E	T	10 E	X	11 T		R	E	T	I	12 N	U	E						
E		E		U		A					V		N			13 S				
R		M		14 I		M		15 N	O		16 A	P	A	T	H	Y				
P		I		G		U		N			C		N			R		17 H	18 I	S
E		N		N		L		Y		19 F	O		M		W			I		M
T		E		O		T				A	U		O		D					P
U		N		M						L	S		U							E
A		T		I						T			S							N
L				N						E										
20 L	U	R	K	I	N	G		21 E	M	B	O	L	D	E	N	E	D			
Y				O				R			L									
		22 C	R	U	C	I	A	L			Y									
		S																		

Across
1. Gave up all resistance
4. Also
6. Belonging to us
8. Neither's partner
9. Excuse
11. Those accompanying a person of rank
15. A negative answer
16. Lack of interest or emotion
17. Belonging to him
20. Exist concealed or unsuspected
21. Encouraged; made brave; gave courage to
22. Critical; of supreme importance

Down
2. Outstanding
3. Absolute power; esp. when used unjustly or cruelly
5. First number
6. Either's partner
7. Lively; spirited
9. Continually
10. Commotion
12. In complete agreement
13. Astute; clever
14. Disgraceful; shameful
18. About to take place
19. Waver in confidence; hesitate; fail

Animal Farm Vocabulary Crossword 3

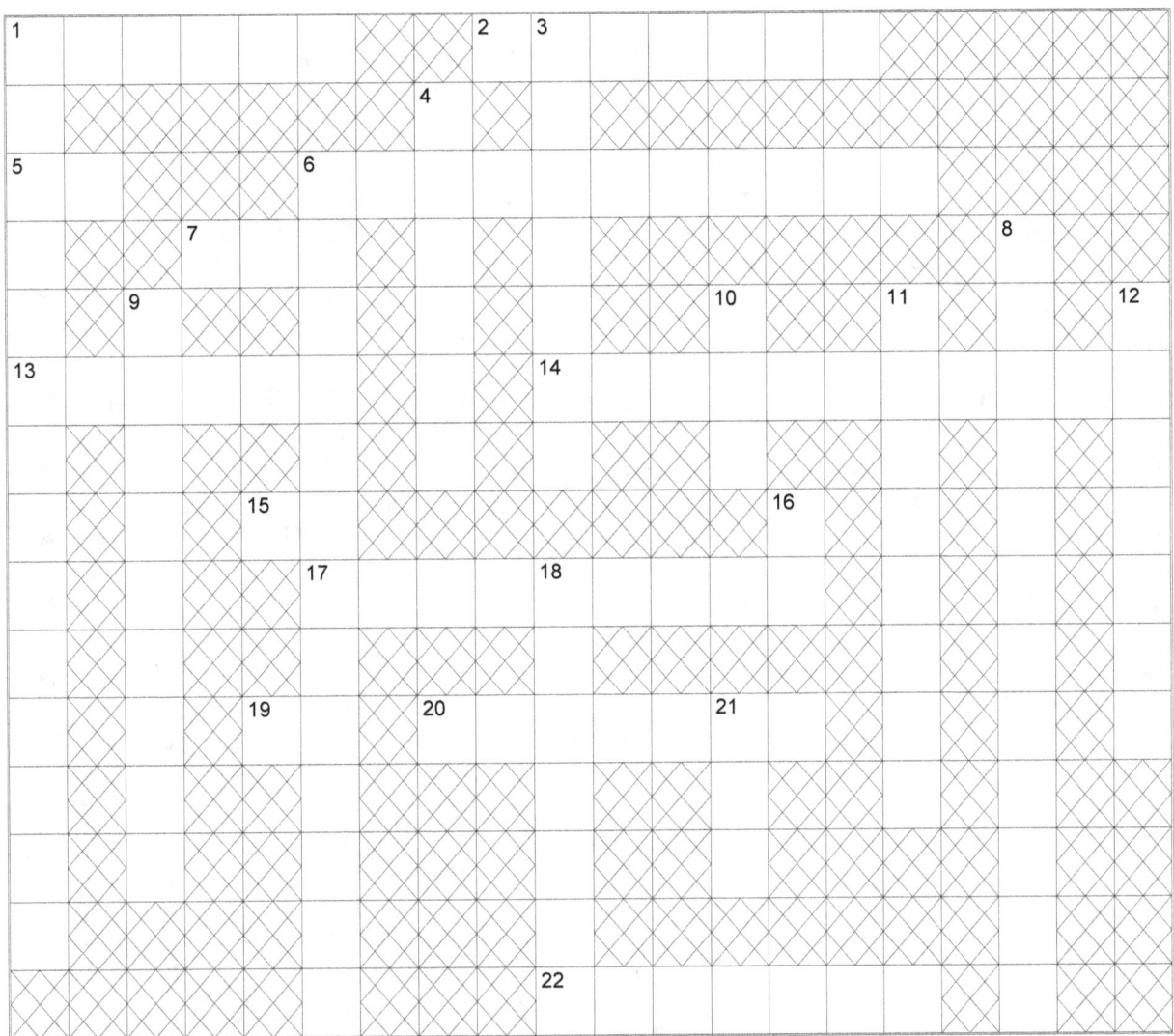

Across
1. Astute; clever
2. Excuse
5. Belonging to me
6. Gave up all resistance
7. Also
13. Commotion
14. In complete agreement
15. A negative answer
17. Lively; spirited
19. Either's partner
20. Sum of money paid as a retirement benefit
22. Exist concealed or unsuspected

Down
1. Happening at the same time
3. Those accompanying a person of rank
4. Lack of interest or emotion
6. Disputes
8. After one's death
9. About to take place
10. A coordinating conjunction
11. Seriously; deeply earnest
12. Absolute power; esp. when used unjustly or cruelly
16. Ourselves
18. Bitterly mocking
21. Belonging to us

Animal Farm Vocabulary Crossword 3 Answer Key

¹S	H	R	E	W	D		²P	³R	E	T	E	X	T
I						⁴A		E					
⁵M	Y			⁶C	A	P	I	T	U	L	A	T	E	D
U			⁷T	O	O		A		I					⁸P
L		⁹I		N		T		N		¹⁰A		¹¹S		O	¹²T
¹³T	U	M	U	L	T		H		¹⁴U	N	A	N	I	M	O	U	S	L	Y
A		P			R		Y		E			D				L		T		R
N		E		¹⁵N	O								¹⁶U		E		H		A
E		N		¹⁷V	I	V	A	¹⁸C	I	O	U	S		M		U		N
O		D		E				Y					N		M		N
U		I		¹⁹O	R		²⁰P	E	N	S	I	²¹O	N		L		O		Y
S		N		S			I					U			Y		U
L		G		I			C					R					S
Y				E			A										L
				S			²²L	U	R	K	I	N	G				Y

Across
1. Astute; clever
2. Excuse
5. Belonging to me
6. Gave up all resistance
7. Also
13. Commotion
14. In complete agreement
15. A negative answer
17. Lively; spirited
19. Either's partner
20. Sum of money paid as a retirement benefit
22. Exist concealed or unsuspected

Down
1. Happening at the same time
3. Those accompanying a person of rank
4. Lack of interest or emotion
6. Disputes
8. After one's death
9. About to take place
10. A coordinating conjunction
11. Seriously; deeply earnest
12. Absolute power; esp. when used unjustly or cruelly
16. Ourselves
18. Bitterly mocking
21. Belonging to us

100
Copyrighted

Animal Farm Vocabulary Crossword 4

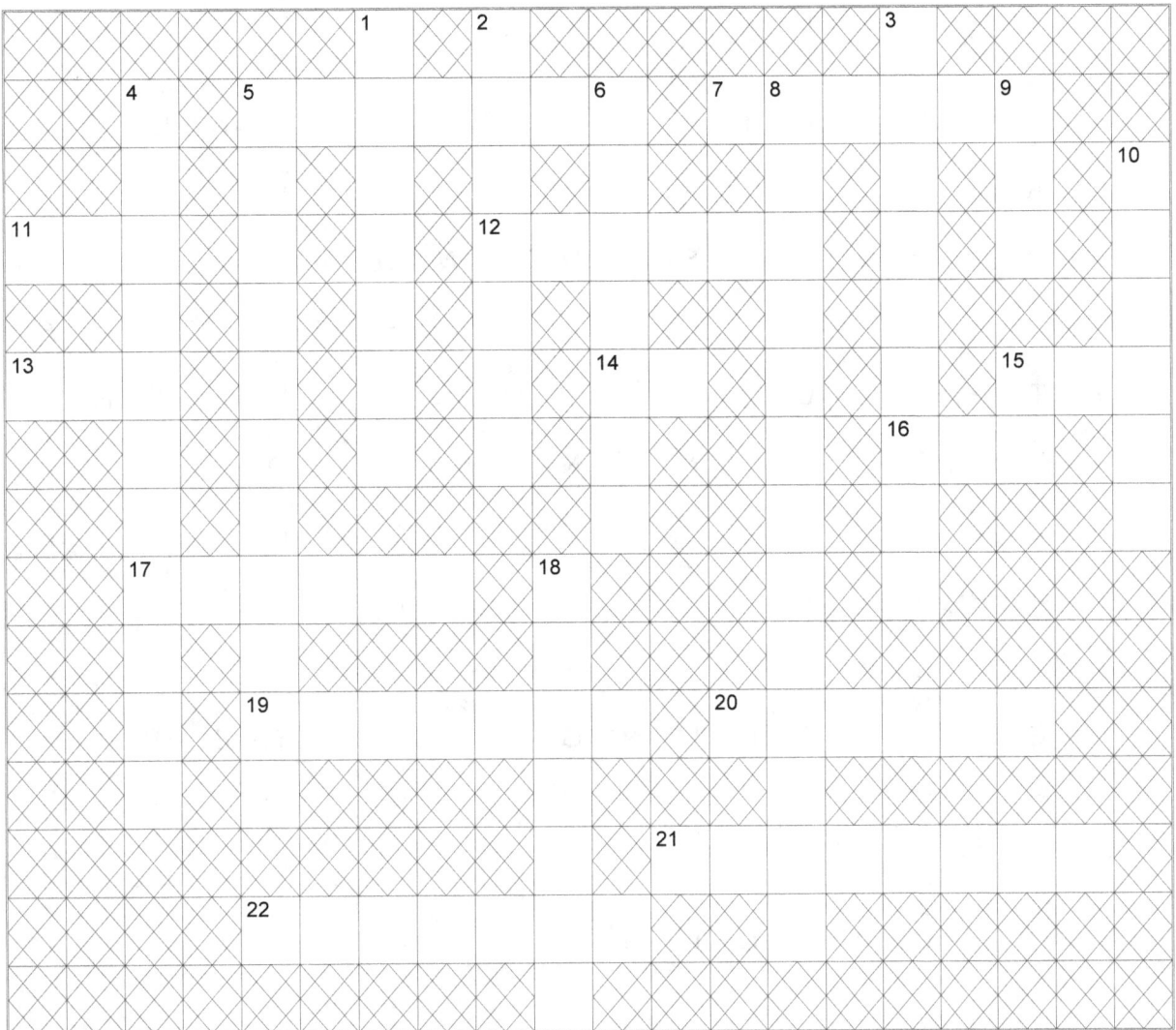

Across
5. Excuse
7. Befitting a son or daughter
11. It can hold hot tea
12. Astute; clever
13. Allow
14. A negative answer
15. First number
16. Belonging to us
17. Lack of interest or emotion
19. Exist concealed or unsuspected
20. Waver in confidence; hesitate; fail
21. Seriously; deeply earnest
22. Critical; of supreme importance

Down
1. Those accompanying a person of rank
2. Sum of money paid as a retirement benefit
3. Lively; spirited
4. Gave up all resistance
5. Continually
6. Absolute power; esp. when used unjustly or cruelly
8. Untiring; tireless
9. A falsehood; an untruth
10. Me
15. Either's partner
18. Bitterly mocking

Animal Farm Vocabulary Crossword 4 Answer Key

			1 R	2 P				3 V		
	4 C	5 P	R	E	T	E	X	T		
					6 T	7 F	8 I	L	I	A	L	9 L	
	A	E	T	N		Y		I	N	V	A	E	10 M

Across
5. Excuse
7. Befitting a son or daughter
11. It can hold hot tea
12. Astute; clever
13. Allow
14. A negative answer
15. First number
16. Belonging to us
17. Lack of interest or emotion
19. Exist concealed or unsuspected
20. Waver in confidence; hesitate; fail
21. Seriously; deeply earnest
22. Critical; of supreme importance

Down
1. Those accompanying a person of rank
2. Sum of money paid as a retirement benefit
3. Lively; spirited
4. Gave up all resistance
5. Continually
6. Absolute power; esp. when used unjustly or cruelly
8. Untiring; tireless
9. A falsehood; an untruth
10. Me
15. Either's partner
18. Bitterly mocking

Animal Farm Vocabulary Juggle Letters 1

1. LYOSMOHPSUUT = 1. _____
   After one's death

2. CYNALIC = 2. _____
   Bitterly mocking

3. IPRNTEEEMN = 3. _____
   Outstanding

4. NLOESMLY = 4. _____
   Seriously; deeply earnest

5. PDNEMIIGN = 5. _____
   About to take place

6. UMTLTU = 6. _____
   Commotion

7. AIFILL = 7. _____
   Befitting a son or daughter

8. ENLMEEDBDO = 8. _____
   Encouraged; made brave; gave courage to

9. TOUSUELNYMCOPT = 9. _____
   Scornfully

10. AUILTETCAPD =10. _____
    Gave up all resistance

11. KGINLRU =11. _____
    Exist concealed or unsuspected

12. DRUUENSEPAANT =12. _____
    Retired because of age or infirmity

13. CONILCARITOY =13. _____
    Showing good-will; peace-making

14. NNCECNOATEU =14. _____
    Facial expression

15. ACUCIRL =15. _____
    Critical; of supreme importance

Animal Farm Vocabulary Juggle Letters 1 Answer Key

1. LYOSMOHPSUUT = 1. POSTHUMOUSLY
   After one's death

2. CYNALIC = 2. CYNICAL
   Bitterly mocking

3. IPRNTEEEMN = 3. PREEMINENT
   Outstanding

4. NLOESMLY = 4. SOLEMNLY
   Seriously; deeply earnest

5. PDNEMIIGN = 5. IMPENDING
   About to take place

6. UMTLTU = 6. TUMULT
   Commotion

7. AIFILL = 7. FILIAL
   Befitting a son or daughter

8. ENLMEEDBDO = 8. EMBOLDENED
   Encouraged; made brave; gave courage to

9. TOUSUELNYMCOPT = 9. CONTEMPTUOUSLY
   Scornfully

10. AUILTETCAPD =10. CAPITULATED
    Gave up all resistance

11. KGINLRU =11. LURKING
    Exist concealed or unsuspected

12. DRUUENSEPAANT =12. SUPERANNUATED
    Retired because of age or infirmity

13. CONILCARITOY =13. CONCILIATORY
    Showing good-will; peace-making

14. NNCECNOATEU =14. COUNTENANCE
    Facial expression

15. ACUCIRL =15. CRUCIAL
    Critical; of supreme importance

Animal Farm Vocabulary Juggle Letters 2

1. OUIRPMPMT = 1. _____
   Not rehearsed; on the spur of the moment

2. TTXEPER = 2. _____
   Excuse

3. LUMUTT = 3. _____
   Commotion

4. YTHAPA = 4. _____
   Lack of interest or emotion

5. ASNUNRPUDEEAT = 5. _____
   Retired because of age or infirmity

6. NCETENAUOCN = 6. _____
   Facial expression

7. OENPINS = 7. _____
   Sum of money paid as a retirement benefit

8. OCTYCOLANIRI = 8. _____
   Showing good-will; peace-making

9. PDMGNINEI = 9. _____
   About to take place

10. AETLFR = 10. _____
    Waver in confidence; hesitate; fail

11. WHRSDE = 11. _____
    Astute; clever

12. RRIELESEPISBR = 12. _____
    Impossible to control or restrain

13. NCSOUMPYLTOUET = 13. _____
    Scornfully

14. AYCCILN = 14. _____
    Bitterly mocking

15. SOOLYUPTSMHU = 15. _____
    After one's death

Animal Farm Vocabulary Juggle Letters 2 Answer Key

1. OUIRPMPMT = 1. IMPROMPTU
   Not rehearsed; on the spur of the moment

2. TTXEPER = 2. PRETEXT
   Excuse

3. LUMUTT = 3. TUMULT
   Commotion

4. YTHAPA = 4. APATHY
   Lack of interest or emotion

5. ASNUNRPUDEEAT = 5. SUPERANNUATED
   Retired because of age or infirmity

6. NCETENAUOCN = 6. COUNTENANCE
   Facial expression

7. OENPINS = 7. PENSION
   Sum of money paid as a retirement benefit

8. OCTYCOLANIRI = 8. CONCILIATORY
   Showing good-will; peace-making

9. PDMGNINEI = 9. IMPENDING
   About to take place

10. AETLFR = 10. FALTER
    Waver in confidence; hesitate; fail

11. WHRSDE = 11. SHREWD
    Astute; clever

12. RRIELESEPISBR = 12. IRREPRESSIBLE
    Impossible to control or restrain

13. NCSOUMPYLTOUET = 13. CONTEMPTUOUSLY
    Scornfully

14. AYCCILN = 14. CYNICAL
    Bitterly mocking

15. SOOLYUPTSMHU = 15. POSTHUMOUSLY
    After one's death

Animal Farm Vocabulary Juggle Letters 3

1. OEYUCMOLUNSPTT = 1. _____
   Scornfully

2. ILECDTPTAAU = 2. _____
   Gave up all resistance

3. OEEOTVNSRS ICR = 3. _____
   Disputes

4. PIPORMUMT = 4. _____
   Not rehearsed; on the spur of the moment

5. RLPSEEBSEIRRI = 5. _____
   Impossible to control or restrain

6. UTCONANENCE = 6. _____
   Facial expression

7. UETIENR = 7. _____
   Those accompanying a person of rank

8. ONEPNIS = 8. _____
   Sum of money paid as a retirement benefit

9. NPAUNUADEETSR = 9. _____
   Retired because of age or infirmity

10. UTULTM = 10. _____
    Commotion

11. AAPYHT = 11. _____
    Lack of interest or emotion

12. CIUIVOAVS = 12. _____
    Lively; spirited

13. OOIISGNIMNU = 13. _____
    Disgraceful; shameful

14. EPMENTNIER = 14. _____
    Outstanding

15. BSTNIIEARE = 15. _____
    Drunkards

Animal Farm Vocabulary Juggle Letters 3 Answer Key

1. OEYUCMOLUNSPTT = 1. CONTEMPTUOUSLY
   Scornfully

2. ILECDTPTAAU = 2. CAPITULATED
   Gave up all resistance

3. OEEOTVNSRS ICR = 3. CONTROVERSIES
   Disputes

4. PIPORMUMT = 4. IMPROMPTU
   Not rehearsed; on the spur of the moment

5. RLPSEEBSEIRRI = 5. IRREPRESSIBLE
   Impossible to control or restrain

6. UTCONANENCE = 6. COUNTENANCE
   Facial expression

7. UETIENR = 7. RETINUE
   Those accompanying a person of rank

8. ONEPNIS = 8. PENSION
   Sum of money paid as a retirement benefit

9. NPAUNUADEETSR = 9. SUPERANNUATED
   Retired because of age or infirmity

10. UTULTM = 10. TUMULT
    Commotion

11. AAPYHT = 11. APATHY
    Lack of interest or emotion

12. CIUIVOAVS = 12. VIVACIOUS
    Lively; spirited

13. OOIISGNIMNU = 13. IGNOMINIOUS
    Disgraceful; shameful

14. EPMENTNIER = 14. PREEMINENT
    Outstanding

15. BSTNIIEARE = 15. INEBRIATES
    Drunkards

Animal Farm Vocabulary Juggle Letters 4

1. BTTOENIAS = 1. _____
   Stubbornly inflexible

2. EDWSRH = 2. _____
   Astute; clever

3. OLTUYPOUHSMS = 3. _____
   After one's death

4. ULPPTERLEAY = 4. _____
   Continually

5. LAIIFL = 5. _____
   Befitting a son or daughter

6. NENPIOS = 6. _____
   Sum of money paid as a retirement benefit

7. NIETENERPM = 7. _____
   Outstanding

8. ADILTECTPUA = 8. _____
   Gave up all resistance

9. NTOPLUMSTYOECU = 9. _____
   Scornfully

10. ICRUALC = 10. _____
    Critical; of supreme importance

11. SERISLEPRRIBE = 11. _____
    Impossible to control or restrain

12. EMOSLLYN = 12. _____
    Seriously; deeply earnest

13. TTLUMU = 13. _____
    Commotion

14. ITRUEEN = 14. _____
    Those accompanying a person of rank

15. GNURKLI = 15. _____
    Exist concealed or unsuspected

Animal Farm Vocabulary Juggle Letters 4 Answer Key

1. BTTOENIAS = 1. OBSTINATE
Stubbornly inflexible

2. EDWSRH = 2. SHREWD
Astute; clever

3. OLTUYPOUHSMS = 3. POSTHUMOUSLY
After one's death

4. ULPPTERLEAY = 4. PERPETUALLY
Continually

5. LAIIFL = 5. FILIAL
Befitting a son or daughter

6. NENPIOS = 6. PENSION
Sum of money paid as a retirement benefit

7. NIETENERPM = 7. PREEMINENT
Outstanding

8. ADILTECTPUA = 8. CAPITULATED
Gave up all resistance

9. NTOPLUMSTYOECU = 9. CONTEMPTUOUSLY
Scornfully

10. ICRUALC =10. CRUCIAL
Critical; of supreme importance

11. SERISLEPRRIBE =11. IRREPRESSIBLE
Impossible to control or restrain

12. EMOSLLYN =12. SOLEMNLY
Seriously; deeply earnest

13. TTLUMU =13. TUMULT
Commotion

14. ITRUEEN =14. RETINUE
Those accompanying a person of rank

15. GNURKLI =15. LURKING
Exist concealed or unsuspected

APATHY	Lack of interest or emotion
CAPITULATED	Gave up all resistance
CONCILIATORY	Showing good-will; peace-making
CONTEMPTUOUSLY	Scornfully
CONTROVERSIES	Disputes
COUNTENANCE	Facial expression

CRUCIAL	Critical; of supreme importance
CYNICAL	Bitterly mocking
EMBOLDENED	Encouraged; made brave; gave courage to
FALTER	Waver in confidence; hesitate; fail
FILIAL	Befitting a son or daughter
IGNOMINIOUS	Disgraceful; shameful

IMPENDING	About to take place
IMPROMPTU	Not rehearsed; on the spur of the moment
INDEFATIGABLE	Untiring; tireless
INEBRIATES	Drunkards
IRREPRESSIBLE	Impossible to control or restrain
LURKING	Exist concealed or unsuspected

OBSTINATE	Stubbornly inflexible
PENSION	Sum of money paid as a retirement benefit
PERPETUALLY	Continually
POSTHUMOUSLY	After one's death
PREEMINENT	Outstanding
PRETEXT	Excuse

RETINUE	Those accompanying a person of rank
SHREWD	Astute; clever
SIMULTANEOUSLY	Happening at the same time
SOLEMNLY	Seriously; deeply earnest
SUPERANNUATED	Retired because of age or infirmity
TUMULT	Commotion

TYRANNY	Absolute power; esp. when used unjustly or cruelly
UNANIMOUSLY	In complete agreement
VIVACIOUS	Lively; spirited

Animal Farm

RETINUE	PENSION	INDEFATIGABLE	TYRANNY	VIVACIOUS
CRUCIAL	UNANIMOUSLY	IMPROMPTU	IMPENDING	PREEMINENT
POSTHUMOUSLY	OBSTINATE	FREE SPACE	CONCILIATORY	FILIAL
LURKING	CYNICAL	CONTEMPTUOUSLY	PERPETUALLY	TUMULT
SIMULTANEOUSLY	INEBRIATES	SOLEMNLY	PRETEXT	COUNTENANCE

Animal Farm

FALTER	CAPITULATED	SHREWD	CONTROVERSIES	IGNOMINIOUS
EMBOLDENED	APATHY	IRREPRESSIBLE	COUNTENANCE	PRETEXT
SOLEMNLY	INEBRIATES	FREE SPACE	TUMULT	PERPETUALLY
CONTEMPTUOUSLY	CYNICAL	LURKING	FILIAL	CONCILIATORY
SUPERANNUATED	OBSTINATE	POSTHUMOUSLY	PREEMINENT	IMPENDING

Animal Farm

OBSTINATE	EMBOLDENED	CONTEMPTUOUSLY	IMPENDING	FILIAL
CYNICAL	RETINUE	TUMULT	TYRANNY	IRREPRESSIBLE
SUPERANNUATED	CONCILIATORY	FREE SPACE	SIMULTANEOUSLY	VIVACIOUS
APATHY	CAPITULATED	COUNTENANCE	POSTHUMOUSLY	PREEMINENT
CONTROVERSIES	SHREWD	LURKING	FALTER	IMPROMPTU

Animal Farm

PERPETUALLY	PENSION	INDEFATIGABLE	CRUCIAL	UNANIMOUSLY
PRETEXT	SOLEMNLY	INEBRIATES	IMPROMPTU	FALTER
LURKING	SHREWD	FREE SPACE	PREEMINENT	POSTHUMOUSLY
COUNTENANCE	CAPITULATED	APATHY	VIVACIOUS	SIMULTANEOUSLY
IGNOMINIOUS	CONCILIATORY	SUPERANNUATED	IRREPRESSIBLE	TYRANNY

Animal Farm

INEBRIATES	PREEMINENT	UNANIMOUSLY	SUPERANNUATED	FILIAL
IRREPRESSIBLE	PERPETUALLY	COUNTENANCE	POSTHUMOUSLY	TUMULT
VIVACIOUS	CRUCIAL	FREE SPACE	SIMULTANEOUSLY	RETINUE
CONTROVERSIES	SHREWD	CONTEMPTUOUSLY	TYRANNY	PENSION
IMPENDING	EMBOLDENED	OBSTINATE	CYNICAL	SOLEMNLY

Animal Farm

IGNOMINIOUS	APATHY	CONCILIATORY	IMPROMPTU	CAPITULATED
INDEFATIGABLE	LURKING	PRETEXT	SOLEMNLY	CYNICAL
OBSTINATE	EMBOLDENED	FREE SPACE	PENSION	TYRANNY
CONTEMPTUOUSLY	SHREWD	CONTROVERSIES	RETINUE	SIMULTANEOUSLY
FALTER	CRUCIAL	VIVACIOUS	TUMULT	POSTHUMOUSLY

Animal Farm

PENSION	TYRANNY	SUPERANNUATED	PERPETUALLY	COUNTENANCE
SHREWD	APATHY	INEBRIATES	EMBOLDENED	POSTHUMOUSLY
UNANIMOUSLY	FILIAL	FREE SPACE	CRUCIAL	INDEFATIGABLE
LURKING	SIMULTANEOUSLY	CAPITULATED	IGNOMINIOUS	IMPROMPTU
VIVACIOUS	SOLEMNLY	RETINUE	CONCILIATORY	FALTER

Animal Farm

IMPENDING	CYNICAL	OBSTINATE	PREEMINENT	IRREPRESSIBLE
CONTROVERSIES	PRETEXT	CONTEMPTUOUSLY	FALTER	CONCILIATORY
RETINUE	SOLEMNLY	FREE SPACE	IMPROMPTU	IGNOMINIOUS
CAPITULATED	SIMULTANEOUSLY	LURKING	INDEFATIGABLE	CRUCIAL
TUMULT	FILIAL	UNANIMOUSLY	POSTHUMOUSLY	EMBOLDENED

Animal Farm

FALTER	OBSTINATE	RETINUE	IMPENDING	CAPITULATED
INEBRIATES	POSTHUMOUSLY	SOLEMNLY	EMBOLDENED	CONTEMPTUOUSLY
APATHY	CYNICAL	FREE SPACE	IGNOMINIOUS	UNANIMOUSLY
PERPETUALLY	LURKING	PRETEXT	IRREPRESSIBLE	CONTROVERSIES
TYRANNY	IMPROMPTU	SIMULTANEOUSLY	CONCILIATORY	VIVACIOUS

Animal Farm

FILIAL	TUMULT	SUPERANNUATED	CRUCIAL	INDEFATIGABLE
PENSION	PREEMINENT	SHREWD	VIVACIOUS	CONCILIATORY
SIMULTANEOUSLY	IMPROMPTU	FREE SPACE	CONTROVERSIES	IRREPRESSIBLE
PRETEXT	LURKING	PERPETUALLY	UNANIMOUSLY	IGNOMINIOUS
COUNTENANCE	CYNICAL	APATHY	CONTEMPTUOUSLY	EMBOLDENED

Animal Farm

POSTHUMOUSLY	SIMULTANEOUSLY	TUMULT	PERPETUALLY	FALTER
CYNICAL	VIVACIOUS	PENSION	CONTEMPTUOUSLY	SOLEMNLY
TYRANNY	INEBRIATES	FREE SPACE	CONCILIATORY	INDEFATIGABLE
IMPROMPTU	PREEMINENT	RETINUE	FILIAL	CONTROVERSIES
SUPERANNUATED	SHREWD	PRETEXT	IRREPRESSIBLE	OBSTINATE

Animal Farm

EMBOLDENED	APATHY	CAPITULATED	CRUCIAL	COUNTENANCE
IGNOMINIOUS	LURKING	UNANIMOUSLY	OBSTINATE	IRREPRESSIBLE
PRETEXT	SHREWD	FREE SPACE	CONTROVERSIES	FILIAL
RETINUE	PREEMINENT	IMPROMPTU	INDEFATIGABLE	CONCILIATORY
IMPENDING	INEBRIATES	TYRANNY	SOLEMNLY	CONTEMPTUOUSLY

Animal Farm

FALTER	CAPITULATED	RETINUE	IMPROMPTU	SIMULTANEOUSLY
INEBRIATES	TUMULT	VIVACIOUS	PREEMINENT	PERPETUALLY
INDEFATIGABLE	CONTEMPTUOUSLY	FREE SPACE	IMPENDING	SUPERANNUATED
SOLEMNLY	UNANIMOUSLY	CRUCIAL	IRREPRESSIBLE	CYNICAL
CONTROVERSIES	IGNOMINIOUS	PENSION	LURKING	CONCILIATORY

Animal Farm

POSTHUMOUSLY	APATHY	EMBOLDENED	PRETEXT	COUNTENANCE
FILIAL	TYRANNY	SHREWD	CONCILIATORY	LURKING
PENSION	IGNOMINIOUS	FREE SPACE	CYNICAL	IRREPRESSIBLE
CRUCIAL	UNANIMOUSLY	SOLEMNLY	SUPERANNUATED	IMPENDING
OBSTINATE	CONTEMPTUOUSLY	INDEFATIGABLE	PERPETUALLY	PREEMINENT

Animal Farm

OBSTINATE	IGNOMINIOUS	IRREPRESSIBLE	FALTER	APATHY
CONTEMPTUOUSLY	FILIAL	CYNICAL	UNANIMOUSLY	CONCILIATORY
POSTHUMOUSLY	IMPROMPTU	FREE SPACE	SHREWD	TYRANNY
EMBOLDENED	INEBRIATES	LURKING	RETINUE	PERPETUALLY
CAPITULATED	SIMULTANEOUSLY	INDEFATIGABLE	IMPENDING	CRUCIAL

Animal Farm

CONTROVERSIES	PRETEXT	SUPERANNUATED	SOLEMNLY	VIVACIOUS
PREEMINENT	TUMULT	PENSION	CRUCIAL	IMPENDING
INDEFATIGABLE	SIMULTANEOUSLY	FREE SPACE	PERPETUALLY	RETINUE
LURKING	INEBRIATES	EMBOLDENED	TYRANNY	SHREWD
COUNTENANCE	IMPROMPTU	POSTHUMOUSLY	CONCILIATORY	UNANIMOUSLY

Animal Farm

TYRANNY	IMPENDING	CONTEMPTUOUSLY	POSTHUMOUSLY	SIMULTANEOUSLY
CONCILIATORY	INEBRIATES	VIVACIOUS	APATHY	PREEMINENT
COUNTENANCE	UNANIMOUSLY	FREE SPACE	FILIAL	CAPITULATED
CONTROVERSIES	SOLEMNLY	OBSTINATE	IRREPRESSIBLE	PENSION
FALTER	PRETEXT	INDEFATIGABLE	CYNICAL	LURKING

Animal Farm

RETINUE	SHREWD	CRUCIAL	IGNOMINIOUS	IMPROMPTU
EMBOLDENED	TUMULT	SUPERANNUATED	LURKING	CYNICAL
INDEFATIGABLE	PRETEXT	FREE SPACE	PENSION	IRREPRESSIBLE
OBSTINATE	SOLEMNLY	CONTROVERSIES	CAPITULATED	FILIAL
PERPETUALLY	UNANIMOUSLY	COUNTENANCE	PREEMINENT	APATHY

Animal Farm

PREEMINENT	INDEFATIGABLE	OBSTINATE	SIMULTANEOUSLY	UNANIMOUSLY
IRREPRESSIBLE	FALTER	CONTEMPTUOUSLY	COUNTENANCE	CYNICAL
LURKING	PENSION	FREE SPACE	SHREWD	EMBOLDENED
FILIAL	IGNOMINIOUS	APATHY	CONTROVERSIES	SUPERANNUATED
VIVACIOUS	IMPENDING	CAPITULATED	RETINUE	PERPETUALLY

Animal Farm

CRUCIAL	IMPROMPTU	CONCILIATORY	SOLEMNLY	TYRANNY
INEBRIATES	PRETEXT	TUMULT	PERPETUALLY	RETINUE
CAPITULATED	IMPENDING	FREE SPACE	SUPERANNUATED	CONTROVERSIES
APATHY	IGNOMINIOUS	FILIAL	EMBOLDENED	SHREWD
POSTHUMOUSLY	PENSION	LURKING	CYNICAL	COUNTENANCE

Animal Farm

SOLEMNLY	RETINUE	UNANIMOUSLY	CONTEMPTUOUSLY	INDEFATIGABLE
SUPERANNUATED	CONCILIATORY	POSTHUMOUSLY	CYNICAL	LURKING
IMPROMPTU	PRETEXT	FREE SPACE	TUMULT	IMPENDING
CRUCIAL	EMBOLDENED	CONTROVERSIES	PERPETUALLY	SIMULTANEOUSLY
PREEMINENT	FALTER	OBSTINATE	VIVACIOUS	INEBRIATES

Animal Farm

COUNTENANCE	FILIAL	IGNOMINIOUS	CAPITULATED	TYRANNY
IRREPRESSIBLE	PENSION	APATHY	INEBRIATES	VIVACIOUS
OBSTINATE	FALTER	FREE SPACE	SIMULTANEOUSLY	PERPETUALLY
CONTROVERSIES	EMBOLDENED	CRUCIAL	IMPENDING	TUMULT
SHREWD	PRETEXT	IMPROMPTU	LURKING	CYNICAL

Animal Farm

POSTHUMOUSLY	SIMULTANEOUSLY	CRUCIAL	IMPROMPTU	FILIAL
CONCILIATORY	CAPITULATED	PRETEXT	VIVACIOUS	IRREPRESSIBLE
IMPENDING	EMBOLDENED	FREE SPACE	CONTEMPTUOUSLY	IGNOMINIOUS
APATHY	OBSTINATE	SUPERANNUATED	INDEFATIGABLE	LURKING
UNANIMOUSLY	PENSION	CYNICAL	TYRANNY	COUNTENANCE

Animal Farm

RETINUE	SHREWD	PERPETUALLY	TUMULT	PREEMINENT
SOLEMNLY	INEBRIATES	FALTER	COUNTENANCE	TYRANNY
CYNICAL	PENSION	FREE SPACE	LURKING	INDEFATIGABLE
SUPERANNUATED	OBSTINATE	APATHY	IGNOMINIOUS	CONTEMPTUOUSLY
CONTROVERSIES	EMBOLDENED	IMPENDING	IRREPRESSIBLE	VIVACIOUS

Animal Farm

CYNICAL	POSTHUMOUSLY	COUNTENANCE	PENSION	INDEFATIGABLE
SHREWD	CONCILIATORY	CRUCIAL	TYRANNY	RETINUE
OBSTINATE	EMBOLDENED	FREE SPACE	APATHY	PREEMINENT
IMPROMPTU	PRETEXT	INEBRIATES	CONTROVERSIES	IGNOMINIOUS
LURKING	SOLEMNLY	IRREPRESSIBLE	PERPETUALLY	VIVACIOUS

Animal Farm

FALTER	SIMULTANEOUSLY	CAPITULATED	CONTEMPTUOUSLY	SUPERANNUATED
FILIAL	TUMULT	IMPENDING	VIVACIOUS	PERPETUALLY
IRREPRESSIBLE	SOLEMNLY	FREE SPACE	IGNOMINIOUS	CONTROVERSIES
INEBRIATES	PRETEXT	IMPROMPTU	PREEMINENT	APATHY
UNANIMOUSLY	EMBOLDENED	OBSTINATE	RETINUE	TYRANNY

Animal Farm

VIVACIOUS	RETINUE	PRETEXT	APATHY	CYNICAL
IRREPRESSIBLE	TYRANNY	UNANIMOUSLY	POSTHUMOUSLY	SHREWD
PERPETUALLY	SOLEMNLY	FREE SPACE	IMPENDING	FILIAL
IGNOMINIOUS	INDEFATIGABLE	IMPROMPTU	SIMULTANEOUSLY	PREEMINENT
FALTER	LURKING	EMBOLDENED	COUNTENANCE	PENSION

Animal Farm

CAPITULATED	INEBRIATES	CONTROVERSIES	CONTEMPTUOUSLY	TUMULT
SUPERANNUATED	CRUCIAL	OBSTINATE	PENSION	COUNTENANCE
EMBOLDENED	LURKING	FREE SPACE	PREEMINENT	SIMULTANEOUSLY
IMPROMPTU	INDEFATIGABLE	IGNOMINIOUS	FILIAL	IMPENDING
CONCILIATORY	SOLEMNLY	PERPETUALLY	SHREWD	POSTHUMOUSLY

Animal Farm

FALTER	EMBOLDENED	SUPERANNUATED	CAPITULATED	INEBRIATES
LURKING	INDEFATIGABLE	CONCILIATORY	IGNOMINIOUS	POSTHUMOUSLY
UNANIMOUSLY	TYRANNY	FREE SPACE	APATHY	CYNICAL
RETINUE	SOLEMNLY	PENSION	IMPROMPTU	SIMULTANEOUSLY
PRETEXT	OBSTINATE	SHREWD	CONTEMPTUOUSLY	CONTROVERSIES

Animal Farm

PREEMINENT	IRREPRESSIBLE	VIVACIOUS	IMPENDING	COUNTENANCE
PERPETUALLY	TUMULT	FILIAL	CONTROVERSIES	CONTEMPTUOUSLY
SHREWD	OBSTINATE	FREE SPACE	SIMULTANEOUSLY	IMPROMPTU
PENSION	SOLEMNLY	RETINUE	CYNICAL	APATHY
CRUCIAL	TYRANNY	UNANIMOUSLY	POSTHUMOUSLY	IGNOMINIOUS

Animal Farm

APATHY	SHREWD	EMBOLDENED	PREEMINENT	CYNICAL
IRREPRESSIBLE	INEBRIATES	INDEFATIGABLE	CRUCIAL	PRETEXT
COUNTENANCE	POSTHUMOUSLY	FREE SPACE	FILIAL	FALTER
SIMULTANEOUSLY	IMPROMPTU	RETINUE	CONTROVERSIES	TYRANNY
LURKING	PENSION	CAPITULATED	VIVACIOUS	SOLEMNLY

Animal Farm

CONCILIATORY	UNANIMOUSLY	TUMULT	IGNOMINIOUS	OBSTINATE
IMPENDING	CONTEMPTUOUSLY	PERPETUALLY	SOLEMNLY	VIVACIOUS
CAPITULATED	PENSION	FREE SPACE	TYRANNY	CONTROVERSIES
RETINUE	IMPROMPTU	SIMULTANEOUSLY	FALTER	FILIAL
SUPERANNUATED	POSTHUMOUSLY	COUNTENANCE	PRETEXT	CRUCIAL